MARIJUANA HYDROPONICS

HIGH-TECH
WATER CULTURE

Daniel Storm

And/Or Books
Berkeley, California

PUBLISHED BY

And/Or Books

An imprint of Ronin Publishing, Inc.
Post Office Box 1035
Berkeley, California 94701

ISBN: 0-914171-07-0

First printing 1987
Third Printing, 1993
Printed in the United States of America

Project Editor	Sebastian Orfali
Production Manager	Ginger Ashworth
Word Processing	Judith Abrams
Cover	Brian Groppe
Illustrations	Jay Vea
Photographs	Daniel Storm

The material herein is intended for information and reference only.
The author and publisher advise against any application of the
procedures herein if they involve breaking the law or any hazard to
persons and/or property. The reader is cautioned about the use of
drugs, and advised to consult a personal physician. However,
we urge readers to support N.O.R.M.A.L. in its efforts to secure
passage of fair marijuana legislation.

Dedication

I would like to thank Bill, Bob, and George for their assistance. Special thanks to Uncle Norm for his technical and editorial advice. Dedicated to Kathy and Kyle, whose constant love and lack of support made this work possible, and to the memory of Diane.

Table of Contents

1. Light   · 1

2. Plant Mineral Nutrition   7

3. Atmosphere   7

4. Temperature   25

5. Vegetative and Reproductive Growth   29

6. Environmental Growth Systems Assimilation   65

Glossary   105

Appendix I   111

Appendix II   115

Preface

The purpose of this book is to provide reference for growing green plants artificially. That is, without the use of natural environmental factors such as the sun, wind, rain for water and humidity, and naturally occurring mineral nutrients.

The water culture presented here is nothing new; it is simply applied with technology that is available today. With this technology, specifically computers, growing plants artificially with the water culture method will become much more economical and efficient.

Along with the water culture technique, details on construction, assembly, and operation procedures for the completion of growth systems, required for controlling artificial plant growth, will be given.

This work also contains basic background information on botanical aspects that are necessary for vigorous, healthy plant growth.

Two significant books related to this area, which should be consulted, are: *Marijuana Botany*, by Robert Connell Clarke, and *Marijuana Grower's Guide*, by Mel Frank and Ed Rosenthal. Both are available from And/Or Books.

1

Light

The size of marijuana plants, their potency, even the time when they produce buds — all these are dependent on the light they receive: its quality, intensity, and duration. This chapter explains how the photoperiod influences the onset of flowering, and how it may be used to induce early budding.

Chlorophyll

Before photosynthesis can begin, radiant energy (i.e., light) absorbed by the plant is converted into chemical energy. This energy transfer occurs within the unique cellular structures called chloroplasts. The basic components of chloroplasts are individual membranous sacs, containing fats, proteins and pigments.

Light-absorbing pigments are attached to the membranes of the sacs. There are several types of pigments; each absorbs different wavelengths of light. The most important plant pigment is chlorophyll. In green plants, chlorophyll occurs in two forms: chlorophyll a and chlorophyll b. Both chlorophyll molecules absorb red and blue wavelengths of light. Green wavelengths of light are reflected, giving plants their characteristic color.

Photosynthesis

When sunlight falls on the leaves of green plants, the illuminating energy triggers the process of photosynthesis.

Along with light and chlorophyll, photosynthesis involves carbon dioxide (CO_2) and water (H_2O). According to current theory on the mechanism of photosynthesis, the chemical energy produced by chlorophyll from visible light is sufficient to split the water molecules apart. This provides units of hydrogen (H), and hydroxide units (OH). The hydroxide units combine with carbon dioxide absorbed from the air, to produce carbohydrates necessary for plant growth. The hydroxide units also become the source of oxygen molecules, which (along with water vapor) are released back into the atmosphere. Here is a summary of the photosynthesis reaction:

$$6CO_2 + 12H_2O \xrightarrow[\text{chlorophyll}]{\text{light}} C_6H_{12}O_6 + 6H_2O + 6O_2$$

(carbon
dioxide) (water)   (glucose)   (water)   (oxygen)

Photorespiration

In the chlorophyllous tissues, both respiration, which occurs in darkness, and photorespiration, which occurs in the presence of light, are carried on continuously throughout the life cycle of the marijuana plant. The reaction involved in respiration is the reverse of that involved in photosynthesis. Carbohydrates produced during photosynthesis are broken down by oxygen, releasing carbon dioxide and water back into the atmosphere, and supplying energy for other plant growth processes. The reaction mechanism for both respiration and photorespiration is:

$$CH_2O + O_2 \xrightarrow[\text{dark}]{\text{light}} CO_2 + H_2O + \text{Energy}$$

(carbohydrate) (oxygen)   (carbon
dioxide)   (water)

Photorespiration proceeds at a slightly higher rate than does respiration. A measure of the rate of photorespiration is called the carbon dioxide compensation point. When this point is reached, the amount of carbon dioxide given off in photorespiration is exactly equal to the amount of carbon dioxide taken in during photosynthesis. At the carbon dioxide compensation point, the net rate of photosynthesis is zero. A plant can increase in growth only if the rate of photosynthesis exceeds the rate of photorespiration. Therefore it is necessary to raise the external concentration of carbon dioxide above the carbon dioxide compensation point to bring about an increase in the rate of photosynthesis. (Ways of doing this will be discussed in Chapter 3.)

Light Intensity

Along with the increase in carbon dioxide concentration, an increase in the intensity of available light reduces the inhibitory effects of photorespiration. The photosynthetic process is said to be light-saturated when the

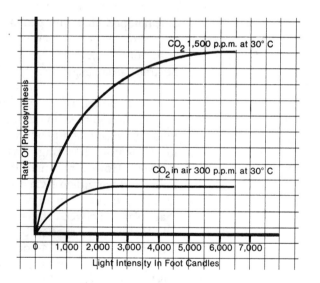

Figure 1.
Shows an increase in the rate of photosynthesis with an increase in the carbon dioxide concentration and light intensity.

rate of photosynthesis will not increase with light intensities above 2,000 footcandles at normal atmospheric concentrations of carbon dioxide. (Sunlight on a clear midsummer day is between 12,000 and 15,000 footcandles.) However, if the concentration of carbon dioxide is increased along with high light intensity, the rate of photosynthesis will also increase (see Figure 1, page 3).

To satisfy these lighting requirements in a growth chamber, high-intensity discharge lamps must be used. A recommended lamp will be described at the end of this chapter.

Photoperiodism

For most types of plants there is a direct relationship between the lengths of the day and night periods and the time in the plant's life cycle when flowering occurs. This relationship is called the photoperiod. This section will deal with the photoperiodic responses of cannabis, which is a short-day plant. (There are three kinds of photoperiodism in plants. Short-day plants will flower with short days and long nights. Long-day plants will flower with long days and short nights. When plants are day-neutral, the daylength does not have any effect on flowering.)

In 1954 two plant physiologists, H. A. Borthwick and W. J. Skully, were trying to find new ways to improve crop yields and breeding techniques for cannabis. According to their findings, when plants were exposed to daylengths of 16 to 20 hours, flowering was incomplete and was greatly delayed. However, when they received daylengths of 18 hours and were then switched to daylengths of 8 to 14 hours, flowering occurred in all plants. The researchers found further that plants between three and five weeks old flowered within two weeks after being changed over from 18-hour daylengths to 8- to 14-hour daylengths. The five-week-old plants required fewer 8- to 14-hour daylengths than the three-week-old plants to produce the same amount of flowering.

One of the most interesting observations related to photoperiodism was the occurrence of "intersexual" flowers on the marijuana plant. They discovered that when plants were exposed to daylengths longer than 16 hours and then changed over to daylengths of 8 to 11 hours, the production of male flowers on female plants ranged from 45 percent to 25 percent respectively for the shorter daylengths. Also, the occurrence of male flowers on female plants that received daylengths of 12 to 14 hours was greatly reduced or completely prevented. Another important observation was that when the female flowers were pollinated from male flowers on the same plant, only seeds that produced female plants resulted. Because of the female plants' potency, this finding is quite valuable to growers.

Plant Growth Lighting

It would be ideal, of course, to be able to use the sun as the primary source of illumination. However, most people cannot afford greenhouses, skylights, or other materials necessary to make adequate use of sunlight. Growth chambers equipped with highly efficient lighting are an economical substitute.

The most effective source of artificial light found to date is the 1,000-watt Lucalox lamp from General Electric, a high-pressure sodium lamp. This lamp has a longer life span, a higher light output, and is more cost-effective than other comparable high-pressure sodium lamps. It is capable of providing a complete and balanced spectrum. If this lamp is housed in its reflector and is maintained at a height between two and four feet above the plants throughout their life cycle, it will produce the high light intensities required for their growth.

References

Arnon, D. I. 1960. "The role of light in photosynthesis." *Scientific American* 203: 105–108.

Borthwick, H. A., S. B. Hendricks, and M. W. Parker. 1952. "The reaction controlling floral initiation." *Botany* 38: 929–933.

Borthwick, H. A. and W. J. Skully. 1954. "Photoperiodic responses of hemp." *Botanical Gazette*: September issue: 14–27.

Burris, R. and C. C. Black. 1975. *CO₂ Metabolism and Plant Productivity*. University Park Press, Baltimore, MD.

Fuller, H. and D. Ritche. Fifth edition, 1967. *General Botany*. Barnes & Noble Books, NY.

General Electric. *Plant Growth Lighting*. TP–127. Others: 220–6111, 205–9307, 206–7343R2, 205–8088, 220–6190R.

Goldsworthy, A. 1970. "Photorespiration." *Botany Review* 36: 321–340.

Govindjee and R. Govindjee. 1974. "The absorption of light in photosynthesis." *Scientific American* 231 (#6): 68–82.

Jackson, W. A. and R. J. Volk. 1970. "Photorespiration." *Annual Review of Plant Physiology* 21: 385–432.

Mark, J. L. 1973. "Photorespiration: key to increasing plant productivity?" *Science* 179: 365–367

Salisbury, F. B. 1963. *The Flowering Process*. Pergamon Press, Inc. Elmsford, NY.

Sylvania. "Horticulture Light Sources." *Engineering Bulletin* 0–352.

Westinghouse. "Agro-Lite." A–8768, A–9045.

2

Plant Mineral Nutrition

To keep plants alive and healthy, a grower needs facts about plant nutrition. This chapter lists all the nutrients a marijuana plant requires, along with their effects; it also explains the diagnosis of plant problems that result from incorrect nutrient concentrations. It analyzes the best nutrient solutions, some useful methods of water purification, the advantages of water culture over other methods of hydroponics, and the effects and importance of proper pH level.

Essential Nutrients

Although many elements are present in cannabis tissues, we will discuss only the essential ones: those necessary for the plant to complete the vegetative, or reproductive, phases of its life cycle. Along with hydrogen, carbon, and oxygen, the six other essential elements, or macronutrients, that are present in the greatest quantities in plants are nitrogen, phosphorus, potassium, calcium, sulfur, and magnesium. Eight other essential elements required in smaller amounts (micronutrients) are iron, boron, manganese, copper, molybdenum, chlorine, zinc, and cobalt. The physiological functions of these elements, as well as the general visible symptoms of deficiencies of the same elements, are given on the following pages.

Macronutrients

Nitrogen

Function: Development of chlorophyll. Promotes stem and fruit growth. Increases protein synthesis. Occurs in amino acids, nucleic acids, enzymes, coenzymes, membranes and other constituents of plant life.

Deficiency: In young plants, stunted growth and yellowish green leaves. Bottom leaves appear light green, followed by yellowing, drying, and shedding, with purplish red pigments in veins. Stems are short and thin; growth is upright and spindly; flowering is reduced.

Phosphorus

Function: Stimulates early root formation. Hastens maturity. Stimulates blooming. Plays a major role in the production of ATP (adenosine triphosphate), a plant energy source. Also found in nucleic acids, fats, coenzymes, and sugar phosphates.

Deficiency: Young plants stunted, leaves dark blue-green, sometimes purplish. Stems thin; veins may show signs of necrosis (blackening and decay of tissues). Plants often dwarf at maturity.

Potassium

Function: Necessary to the formation and transfer of starches, sugars, and oils in the plant. Needed as a cofactor for more than forty enzymes. Performs a vital function in the stomatal movements. (Stomates are structures, found on the leaves, which allow for the exchange of gases and water vapor with the air. See Chapter 3.) Improves seed quality.

Deficiency: Leaves usually dark blue-green with marginal chlorosis (failure to produce normal amounts of chlorophyll). Necrosis, appearing first on bottom leaves; a wrinkled or corrugated appearance between the veins.

Calcium

Function: Influences absorption of plant nutrients. Neutralizes acidic conditions. Neutralizes toxic compounds produced in the plants. Necessary for the development of roots. Component of cell walls. Needed as a coenzyme for the breakdown of ATP and phospholipids.

Deficiency: Leaves chlorotic, rolled, curled. Breakdown of growing tissues in the stem and roots. Roots poorly developed and may appear gelatinous.

Sulfur

Function: Component of amino acids, some fats, proteins, enzymes, coenzymes, and other cellular compounds.

Deficiency: Leaves light green to yellow in color, starting along the veins of the top leaves. Thin stems.

Magnesium

Function: Necessary for a large number of enzymes involved in phosphate transfer. Component of the chlorophyll molecule.

Deficiency: Spotted chlorosis with veins green and leaf web tissue yellow or white, appearing first on the bottom leaves. In severe cases the leaves may wilt and shed; brittleness is common; necrosis usually occurs.

Micronutrients

Iron

Function: Occurs in many of the respiratory enzymes and activates others.

Deficiency: White chlorosis between the veins in the leaves, first on the bottom leaves, often becoming necrotic; leaves may become completely white with brown margins and tips.

Boron

Function: Involved in carbohydrate transport. Necessary for root development. Reduces oxygen uptake by ground leaf tissue.

Deficiency: Top leaves necrotic, shed; growing tissues break down and may become necrotic; roots short and stunted; flowering reduced.

Manganese

Function: Required for the activity of enzymes in photosynthetic production of oxygen.

Deficiency: Spotted chlorosis with leaf web tissue yellow or white, appearing first on the top leaves. Stems yellow, often woody.

Copper

Function: Found in some enzymes, activates others, particularly those enzymes connected with respiration and the chloroplasts.

Deficiency: Wilting of the top leaves, often followed by death; chlorophyll and other pigments reduced.

Molybdenum

Function: Necessary to enzymes and for the breakdown of nitrogen.

Deficiency: Light yellow chlorosis; leaves may fail to develop.

Chlorine

Function: Involved in the photosynthetic reactions for the release of oxygen.

Deficiency: Wilting of the leaf tips with chlorosis and necrosis at the bottom of the wilted area.

Zinc

Function: Component of numerous enzymes.

Deficiency: Leaves chlorotic and necrotic, with the top leaves affected first; shedding; whitish chlorosis between the veins of the bottom leaves.

Cobalt

Function: A component of the Vitamin B_{12} complex (coenzyme).

Deficiency: Top leaves chlorotic; roots considerably reduced.

Nutrient Solution Formulas

For growth to be optimal in water culture, the essential elements must be supplied in a soluble form, with very narrow ranges of concentration for each element. We will now discuss nutrient solutions that fulfill both of these requirements.

Many nutrient solutions have been developed since the first investigations into plant mineral nutrition. Listed here are the recipes that have a good balanced mineral concentration, composition, pH, and solubility for many different varieties of cannabis.

All of these nutrient solutions have been tested and found very effective in growing most varieties of cannabis. However, cannabis responds best to Dr. Chatelier's formula, which has the additional advantage of being premixed so that it can simply be added to water. It is also specifically formulated for exceptionally high solubility.

Arnon/Hoagland (1940)

Macronutrients	Grams per Liter
Potassium Nitrate (KNO_3)	1.02
Calcium Nitrate ($Ca(NO_3)_2$)	0.49
Ammonium Dihydrogen Phosphate ($NH_44H_2PO_4$)	0.23
Magnesium Sulfate ($MgSo_4 \cdot 7H_2O$)	0.49

Micronutrients	Milligrams per Liter
Boric Acid (H_3BO_3)	2.86
Manganese Chloride ($MnCl_2 \cdot 4H_2O$	1.81
Cuprous Sulfate ($CuSo_4 \cdot 5H_2O$)	0.08
Zinc Sulfate ($ZnSo_4 \cdot 7H_2O$)	0.22
Molybdic Acid ($MoO_3 \cdot H_2O$)	0.09

Crone (1902)

Macronutrients	Grams per Liter
Potassium Nitrate (KNO_3)	0.75
Calcium Nitrate ($Ca(NO_3)_2$)	0.25
Calcium Sulfate ($CaSo_4 \cdot 2H_2O$)	0.50
Magnesium Sulfate ($MgSo_4 \cdot 7H_2O$)	0.50

Micronutrients

Same as Arnon/Hoagland (1940)

Dr. Chatelier (1938)

Macronutrients	Percent by Weight
Nitrate Nitrogen	6.00
Ammoniacal Nitrogen	2.00
Phosphoric Acid (P_2O_5)	8.00
Potash (K_2O)	20.00
Calcium	4.00
Magnesium	4.00

Micronutrients*	
Cobalt	.002
Iron	.150
Manganese	.060
Molybdenum	.002

* Note that chlorine, zinc, and copper are missing from this nutrient solution. By using tap water, as described at the end of this chapter, adequate concentrations of these elements may be supplied.

Dr. Chatelier's nutrient formula is quite economical: an eight-ounce bag will produce 128 gallons of solution. (If the reader cannot locate the formula by other means, it can be obtained by writing to me in care of the company listed at the end of this book.)

When using Crone's (or Arnold and Hoagland's) solution, it is easiest first to calculate the number of liters required for the total amount of solution to be prepared. By multiplying the grams and milligrams (1,000 milligrams = 1 gram) per liter by the total number of liters, a more workable number for the weight of each mineral can be obtained.

All solutions mentioned above should have their iron content raised by adding one milliliter of FeEDTA per liter of water. EDTA (ethylenediaminetetraacetic acid) is an organic compound which will bind with Fe (iron) and keep it in solution.

The recipe for FeEDTA is as follows:

A. Dissolve 26.2 grams of EDTA in 413.4 milliliters of distilled water heated to 70 degrees centigrade, with 283.6 milliliters of 1 normal potassium hydroxide (KOH), then add 283.6 milliliters of 1 normal potassium hydroxide.

B. Dissolve 24.9 grams of ferrous sulfate ($FeSo_4 \cdot 7H_2O$) in 300 milliliters of water heated to 70 degrees centigrade, then add 4 milliliters of 1 normal sulfuric acid (H_2SO_4).

C. Mix A and B together and aerate for 24 hours. Add distilled water to the solution to obtain 1 liter.

This solution will yield an initial pH of between 4.0 and 5.0, somewhat below the nutrient solution's reported pH value of 5.5. However, since the FeEDTA will be present in such small amounts, it will not affect the overall pH of the nutrient solution.

pH

The most effective pH range for optimal growth lies between 5 and 7. Cannabis thrives at a pH of 6; however, the influence on cannabis of a pH that is as low as 5, or as high as 7, will be minimal, provided that iron remains available to the plant.

Extremely high or low pH ranges can seriously injure root tissues and reduce the growth rate. Severe injury to the roots is caused by pH values of 3.5 or below, and 9.0 or above. Depression of growth usually starts below 4.5 and above 8.0, as does suppressed seed germination. Mineral deficiencies are also evident over high and low pH ranges (at pH values below 4.0, calcium and potassium are particularly affected). At a pH of 8.0 or higher, calcium, phosphorus, manganese, and iron readily precipitate out of the nutrient solution (and become unavailable to · the plant). Iron, if provided in the form of FeEDTA, will remain in solution at higher pH values. Water cultures maintained at a pH of 7.0 will cause precipitation of calcium and phosphorus if adequate aeration and circulation are not supplied.

The stability of pH depends on several factors, but the most important are renewal of solution, circulation, and aeration. When these conditions are adequate, the pH will remain constant within a + .5 pH range throughout the life cycle of the plant. This is especially true for cannabis. Renewal of the nutrient solution may not become necessary for the first three weeks; however, daily checks of the pH should be made during this period. During the rest of the life cycle, checking the pH is unnecessary, since renewal becomes quite frequent (a single plant will consume roughly 1/2 to 1 gallon of solution per day). The other two factors, circulation and aeration, will be discussed later in detail. (For further information on pH changes in nutrient solution, see the work of E. J. Hewitt, cited at the end of this chapter.)

Sometimes it becomes necessary to adjust the solution to obtain the proper pH. The easiest way is to add 1 normal sodium hydroxide, or 1 normal sulfuric acid. The hydroxide will raise the pH; the acid will lower it. Either one should be added one milliliter at a time until the desired pH is reached.

There are many ways to check the pH of the nutrient solution, but pH paper is the cheapest accurate way. Paper that is graduated in increments of .5, from a range of 4.0 to 8.0, is all you need.

Remember to discard or adjust nutrient solution that measures below 5.0 or above 7.0.

Water

Water is one of the most important factors in the success or failure of a water culture. Natural sources of water include rivers, lakes, wells, and rainwater. Tap, distilled, and demineralized water are the artificial sources.

Demineralized water is the purest water necessary for purposes of water culture. The mineral impurities of water can be removed by passing water through activated charcoal and dacron filters. (The design and construction of a demineralizing device based on these principles will be described in the final chapter of this book, under the heading Water Culture and Aeration Systems.) The filters should be replaced after every 50 gallons of water. The mineral content of water treated in this way has not been determined precisely, but such water always produces excellent results. This device will sufficiently reduce toxic levels of heavy metals if these are present.

Distilled water is ideal for water culture, but its cost is fairly high. Distilled water is usually pure, but contamination may occur depending on the type of still in which it is produced. Generally, stills today are made of stainless steel. If other kinds of metal are used for the still, impurities of copper, zinc, iron, and heavy metals (such as nickel or lead) may be present. It is a good idea to check with the distributor as to the kind of still used. These impurities seldom reach toxic levels, but a knowledge of their presence can still be useful when adjusting the concentration of a particular element in the nutrient solution. Home-sized stills are available, but the expense outweighs their advantages.

Rainwater is a good source, but air pollution must be carefully considered. The pollution contained in the water drops sharply with increasing distance from urban areas. Surprisingly, light rain contains more contaminants than heavy rain. (For further information on this point, the reader may consult the work of E. J. Hewitt, cited at the end of this chapter.) If rainwater is passed through the demineralizing device mentioned above, it becomes excellent for use in water culture solutions.

Tap water contains the largest amount of contaminants. Toxic levels of aluminum, iodine, nickel, and chromium may be present. Free chlorine and fluorine may be injurious if present in high concentrations. However, when tap water is run through a demineralizing device, it too becomes a good and economical water source without any adverse effects on plant growth.

Water Culture or Other Hydroponics Methods?

The water culture technique is one of the methods of hydroponics. It involves suspending plant roots in a solution of water and inorganic materials. This differs from the more commonly known hydroponic method, in which the roots are placed in inert media, such as gravel, sand, or pumice, which provide anchorage for support of the plant. Water culture has many definite advantages over hydroponics.

The use of the water culture technique permits precise control of the supply of nutrients in the root environment. Nutrients and water are always available to the plant. The solution is continuously aerated to supply the roots with oxygen. This prevents carbon dioxide (which is produced by the roots) from reaching toxic levels, and is essential for normal root growth. Adequate aeration cannot be supplied by hydroponic systems. Not only does carbon dioxide reach toxic levels, but air stagnation occurs as well, severely reducing mineral uptake.

Water culture also allows for the maintenance of a constant pH. In hydroponics this is particularly difficult to achieve, due to the precipitation of minerals in the media around the roots. Solution temperatures, and consequently root temperatures, are much easier to control in water culture than in hydroponics.

Another disadvantage of hydroponics is contamination. The inert media are continuously exposed to light and air, which not only contributes to microelement contamination from dust, but provides an excellent breeding ground for algae, bacteria, and fungi. Algae are the most commonly encountered contaminant. These small plants secrete compounds — mainly amino acids — that become activated by light and seriously stunt plant growth.

One more factor to be considered is contamination by carbon dioxide as it is delivered to the atmosphere around the plant. In hydroponic systems, when the nutrient solution enters the growth container and moves from top to bottom, air (which contains dangerous levels of carbon dioxide) is drawn down into the media surrounding the roots. Water culture containers, however, are tightly closed to prevent contact with light and air, which in addition prevents water loss from evaporation.

Introduction to the Water Culture Systems

For water culture to be successful, circulation and renewal of the nutrient solution are of vital importance. Circulation provides the mechanism for keeping the minerals suspended in solution. It also allows movement of the nutrients and oxygen across root tissues. In a continuously circulating system, a constant-level device or a large solution reservoir must be used to insure that an adequate renewal of solution is supplied during the photoperiod, to compensate for the amount lost through the process of transpiration (see Chapter 3). The system that has been used most extensively is shown in Figure 2.

With System #1, a plastic barrel with a 5- to 10-gallon capacity (A) is used for the nutrient solution reservoir tank. This feeds the solution through the float valve (B) into the constant-level tank (C). When demand for solution increases, the valve opens to provide more solution, and the water pump (D) moves it into the growth tanks (E and F). The solution enters at the bottom of each growth tank and exits through the solution return hose (G) at the top. It then moves (using the siphoning effect of gravity) back into the constant-level tank, and is ready to go through the cycle again. By keeping the top of the constant-level tank even with the bottoms of the growth tanks on the air circulation platform (H), a sufficient distance between the tops of the growth tanks and the top of the constant-level tank is maintained to allow for the siphon effect. Aeration is supplied by the air pump (I). Air passes through the air valve (J) and into the air hoses and air stones (K and L).

An alternative method separates the nutrient solution reservoir tank and the constant-level tank. The constant-level tank for this system should have a six- to eight-gallon capacity for supplying up to four growth tanks. Be sure to keep the top of the constant-level tank even with the bottoms of the growth tanks by adjusting the height of the air circulation platform. This method eliminates the need for a float valve in the system.

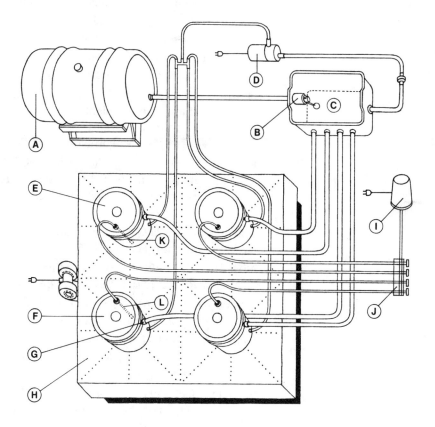

Figure 2.
Water Culture System.

References

Altman, P. L. and D. S. Ditter. 1968. *Metabolism.* Federation of American Societies for Experimental Biology, Bethesda, MD.

Arnon, D. I. and P. R. Stout. 1939. "The essentiality of certain elements in minute quantity for plants with special reference to copper." *Plant Physiology* 14: 371–375.

Arnon, D. I. and D. R. Hoagland. 1938. "The water culture method for growing plants without soil." *Calif. Agr. Exp. Sta.* Cir. 347. Berkeley, CA.

Boyer, T. C., A. B. Carlton, C. M. Johnson and P. R. Stout. 1954. "Chlorine — a micronutrient element for higher plants." *Plant Physiology* 29: 526–532.

Epstein, E. 1972. *Mineral Nutrition of Plants: Principles and Perspectives.* John Wiley & Son, Inc., NY.

Gauch, H. G. 1972. *Inorganic Plant Nutrition.* Dowden, Hutchinson and Ross, Inc., Stroudsburg, PA.

Hewitt, E. 1966. "Sand and water culture methods used in the study of plant nutrition." *Commonwealth Agriculture Bureaux Technical Communication* No. 22, rev. 2nd ed. Fornham Royal, England.

Kirkorian, A. D. and F. C. Steward. 1968. "Water and solutes in plant nutrition: with special references to Van Helmound and Nicholas of Cusa." *Bioscience* 18: 286–292.

Mulder, E. G. 1950. "Mineral nutrition of plants." *Annual Review of Botany* 1: 1–24.

Nicholas, D. J. 1961. "Minor Mineral Nutrients." *Annual Review of Plant Physiology* 12: 63–90.

Schutte, K. H. 1964. *The Biology of Trace Elements.* J.B. Lippincott Co., Philadelphia, PA.

Steiner, A. A. and H. Van Winden. 1970. "Recipe for the ferric salts of ethylenediaminetetraacetic acid." *Plant Physiology* 46: 862–863.

Sutcliffe, J. F. 1962. *Mineral Salt Absorption in Plants.* Pergamon Press, London, England.

Wilson, S. B. and D. J. Nicholas. 1967. "A cobalt requirement for non-nodulated legumes and for wheat phytochemistry." *Phytochem.* 6: 1057–1066.

3

Atmosphere

Every plant needs air to grow. But what are the best atmospheric conditions for a marijuana plant, and how can they be achieved? This chapter covers the most important factors: optimization of humidity, carbon dioxide and oxygen levels, temperature, and air circulation. It also examines the significant effects of carbon dioxide concentration and root aeration, and explains how these may be controlled to produce the best possible plants.

Stomates

Stomates are structures through which plants make contact with the atmosphere. Stomates are numerous small pores in the epidermis of leaves, stems, fruits, and flowers. On leaves, they appear more on the undersurface than on top. Surrounding each stomate are two elongated cells, known as guard cells. These specialized cells provide the mechanical means for opening and closing the stomates. The mechanisms involved in this opening and closure are still widely at issue, but certainly two contributing factors are CO_2 concentration and water stress. (These factors will be discussed in later sections.)

The stomates have two important functions. One is the exchange of gases with the air. Carbon dioxide is drawn into the leaves for photosynthesis, and the oxygen produced is released into the air, through the stomates. The other function, which occurs simultaneously, is the release of water vapor from the leaves. Under normal field conditions this

19

water loss would interfere with optimal growth. However, with the water culture, this becomes a most beneficial effect. (This will be discussed further in the next section.)

Transpiration

The movement of water within plants is one of the most important processes in botany. It is still not clearly known how water flows up and out of the plant, but the transpiration-cohesion theory offers some explanation. When water evaporates from the stomates on the leaves (transpiration), a water shortage is created within the leaves. As a result, water is pulled up through the plant to compensate for the amount lost in transpiration. (This creates a continuous cycle in which water is absorbed and released back into the atmosphere.) The pulling effect results from the cohesion, or "sticking together," of the water molecules. Attraction between the molecules is sufficient to pull water up the stem from the roots and on into the leaves.

Transpiration performs three major functions. First is the flow of water through the plant; second, the delivery of minerals; third, the cooling of the leaves and other organs by the evaporation of the water.

Water flow depends on the rate of transpiration. During the reproductive phase of growth, with relatively high temperatures and low humidity in the growth chamber (see Chapter 5), adequate water flow is critical. Under normal conditions, such temperatures and humidity would be extremely harmful, simply because water could not be absorbed from the soil fast enough, and permanent wilting or thermal death could occur. However, water culture allows for immediate absorption of water to guarantee that transpiration will continue at an optimal rate.

Transpiration also provides a mechanism for the delivery of minerals to the rapidly growing shoot tissues. When water moves up through the plant, the minerals it contains are absorbed by the newly-forming tissues as fast as they can be delivered. The mineral concentration within the plant then becomes low by comparison with that of the nutrient solution surrounding the roots; this allows more minerals to move into the roots along with the water necessary for transpiration. This is why careful maintenance of the correct concentrations of minerals is so important.

The ability of the plant to transpire is essential for the prevention of thermal death. Transpiration is a diffusion process, with the water molecules moving from the leaves (an area of high water vapor concentration) into the air (an area of lower water vapor concentration). Since water is a good thermal conductor, the heat is dissipated into the air with the water vapor. (For more information on water's high heat of vaporization, the reader may wish to consult the work of G. J. Fritz and R. G. Noggle, cited at the end of this chapter.)

Many environmental factors, both external and internal, influence the rate of transpiration. However, the three environmental factors that have the greatest effect on transpiration are air movement, temperature, and relative humidity.

As transpiration occurs, water molecules gather around the openings of the stomates. When air moves across the surfaces of the leaves, the water escapes into the air. Not only is air movement important for removing water vapor; it also brings carbon dioxide into contact with the stomates. It has been estimated that transpiration proceeds twenty times as fast in moving air as it does in still air. However, raising the air velocity past a certain point does not increase the rate of transpiration. (Moreover, as plants become larger, supporting them in high air velocities becomes very difficult.) Therefore, a gentle breeze is most effective in removing water vapor.

Air circulation through growth chambers has posed a few engineering problems, but these have been solved. (A detailed air circulation system will be described in Chapter 5.)

Temperature exerts a drastic influence on the rate of transpiration. With an increase in temperature, water moves from the leaf cells to the stomates, where it is then removed into the atmosphere. However, as we have mentioned, if the temperature rises too high, it may cause thermal injury or death. On the other hand, if the temperature is too low, adequate transpiration will not occur. (Optimal temperatures for total growth responses and transpiration rates will be given in the next chapter.)

Relative humidity is the water vapor content of the air. It is also the controlling factor in transpiration. Most greenhouse growers feel that high relative humidities give better growth results. However, it has been found that high humidity only decreases the amount of water used during transpiration. Other than that, it has no significant effect on growth. It is for this reason that humidity is used to control the rate of water flow through the plant during transpiration. Since our discussion has been focused on the growing of marijuana, we will investigate in Chapter 5 the fact that by modifying relative humidity and other environmental factors, it is possible to control the rate of transpiration and therefore the growth rate, and influence the production of THC in the plant.

Carbon Dioxide

The ability of plants to produce carbohydrates from inorganic materials is the most significant difference between plants and animals. Carbohydrates can be divided into three basic food groups, all of which contain carbon, hydrogen, and oxygen. Production of carbohydrates in plants takes place in order to supply energy (sugars), build cell walls (cellulose), and provide food storage (starch). Some carbohydrates (the sugars) are water-soluble, while others (starch and cellulose) are not. The most common carbohydrates are sucrose ($C_{12}H_{22}O_{11}$), glucose ($C_6H_{12}O_6$), and starch, which consists of chains of glucose units.

Incorrect carbon dioxide concentration is frequently the factor that keeps photosynthesis from proceeding at its maximum rate, and therefore limits the production of carbohydrates as well. This is because the concentration of CO_2 in the atmosphere is .03 percent or 300 ppm (parts per million), which is far below the optimal amount that plants can use. However, an increase in the carbon dioxide concentration to levels above 3,000 ppm produces inhibitory effects. This is largely due to the increased production of carbonic acid, which results in a reduction in pH. The reduction of pH causes closure of the stomates, and CO_2 can no longer be absorbed from the air. From experiments with cannabis, a CO_2 concentration of 1,300 ppm (or 1,000 ppm above normal atmospheric concentrations) produces an increase in photosynthesis and carbohydrate production.

It is also necessary to examine calculation of the growth chamber volume, and of the delivery rate of the gas regulator, to determine the precise amount of CO_2 required. This will be discussed in the final chapter.

Root Atmosphere

Oxygen is essential for normal root development. In nature, when rain is absorbed into the ground, oxygen is drawn down around the roots. With water culture, oxygen must be supplied continuously by aeration. This is done by the use of an aquarium air pump. (The final chapter of this book will describe a complete aeration system.)

Lack of aeration leads to root rot and infections, impedes new root formations, and increases the excretion of organic compounds (such as carboxylic acid, which reduces pH). Moreover, with insufficient aeration, it is impossible for ammoniacal nitrogen, calcium nitrate, and potassium to be absorbed properly. Iron deficiency may also result. Accumulation of carbon dioxide, excreted by the roots in non-aerated solutions, depresses absorption of nutrients and water, which leads to stunting and to abnormal enlargement of the roots.

Aeration is essential to any successful water culture technique.

References

Black, C. C. 1970. "Net carbon dioxide assimilation in higher plants." Proceedings of a symposium of the southern section of the American Society of Plant Physiologists. Cotton Inc., Raleigh, NC.

Fritz, G. J, and R. G. Noggle. 1976. *Introductory Plant Physiology.* Prentice-Hall, Inc., Englewood Cliffs, NJ.

Gates, D. M. 1966. "Transpiration and energy exchange." *Quarterly Review of Biology* 41: 353–364.

Gates, D. M. 1968. "Transpiration and leaf temperature." *Annual Review of Plant Physiology* 19: 211–238.

Goss, J. A. 1973. *Physiology of Plants and Their Cells.* Pergamon Press Inc., NY.

Greulach, V. A. 1973. *Plant Function and Structure.* MacMillan and Co., NY.

Hatch, M. D. and C. R. Slack. 1970. "Photosynthetic CO_2 — fixation pathways." *Annual Review of Plant Physiology* 21: 141–162.

Jarman, P. D. 1974. "The diffusion of CO_2 and water vapor through the stomata." *Journal of Experimental Botany* 25: 927–936.

Raschke, K. and Margret Fellows. 1971. "Stomatal movement in Zea Mays." *Planta* 101: 296–316.

Stiles, W. 1969. *The Principles of Plant Physiology.* 3rd ed. Methuen and Co. Ltd., London, England.

Went, F. E. 1957. *Experimental Control of Plants.* Chronica Botanica Co., Mattham, MA.

Zelitch, I. 1969. "Stomatal control." *Annual Review of Plant Physiology* 20: 329–348.

4

Temperature

Along with light and humidity, temperature is one of the most important factors in the growth of marijuana. This chapter provides experimentally verified day and night temperatures that work best for marijuana plants, including both atmospheric and growth solution temperatures.

Temperature

Temperature has a tremendous effect on plant growth through its influence on the biophysical and biochemical reactions of metabolism. In general, the optimal temperature is that of the plant's natural environment. Although an increase in temperature usually brings about an increase in the reaction rates of metabolism, temperatures above 45 degrees centigrade cause enzyme inactivity, and above 55–60 degrees centigrade protein denaturation occurs, resulting in injury or death.

All varieties of cannabis originate in temperate or tropical climates. Plants from temperate regions have an optimal daytime temperature of about 25–30 degrees centigrade. Tropical plants have the same optimal daytime temperature, but they cannot withstand the extreme temperatures experienced by temperate-climate plants. Tropical temperatures vary only slightly during the growing season.

Plant physiologists have also discovered that optimal nighttime temperatures differ from those that are optimal during the day. This phenomenon, known as thermoperiodicity, results from the fact that organic substances, produced through photosynthesis, move faster at lower temperatures (because sugars are more concentrated at lower temperatures), while cell division and enlargement occur at higher temperatures. It has been found that a photoperiod temperature of 30 degrees centigrade and a nighttime temperature of 22.2 degrees centigrade, maintained throughout the vegetative and reproductive phases, work very well for both temperate and tropical plants. A temperature variation of a few degrees in either direction will not produce any significant effects.

Few studies have been conducted on the optimal temperatures for proper root growth. Generally, the best results have been obtained when the root temperature is a few degrees below the air temperature. It has been found that a solution temperature of 25 degrees centigrade stimulates vigorous root growth. However, more research is needed in this area.

Since all temperatures given here are on the Celsius scale, the following conversion method may be useful:

To convert degrees Fahrenheit to degrees Celsius, subtract 32 from the Fahrenheit figure; multiply the result by 5 and divide by 9.

To convert degrees Celsius to degrees Fahrenheit, multiply the Celsius figure by 9 and divide by 5, then add 32.

References

Bieleski, R. L., A. R. Ferguson, and M. M. Cresswell. 1974. "Mechanisms of regulation of plant growth." *Bull. 12.* The Royal Society of New Zealand, Wellington.

Gates, D. M. 1972. *Man and His Environment: Climate.* Harper & Row, Inc., NY.

Goss, J. A. 1973. *Physiology of Plants and Their Cells.* Pergamon Press Inc., NY.

Greulach, V. A. 1973. *Plant Function and Structure.* MacMillan and Co., NY.

Heslop-Harrison, Y. and I. Woods. 1959. "Temperature induced and other variations in Cannabis sativa." *L. Linn. Soc. Lond. Bot.* 55: 290–293.

Nelson, C. H. 1944. "Growth responses of hemp to different soil and air temperatures." *Plant Physiology* 19: 294–307.

Walker, J. M. 1969. "One degree increments in soil temperature affect in maize seeding behavior." *Soil Sci. Soc. Amer. Proc.* 33: 729.

5

Vegetative and Reproductive Growth

How do marijuana plants actually grow? This chapter explains the growth process in detail, and tells how growers select, store, and germinate marijuana seeds; how they trim the plant for better growth; how they determine the sex of plants. It covers techniques for influencing resin production; methods of curing; and a step-by-step procedure for extracting and refining THC from the leaves that would otherwise be useless. Also featured are actual computer programs that help monitor the development of plants as they grow.

Life Cycle

As with all seed plants, the life cycle of cannabis evolved through the process of alternation of generations.

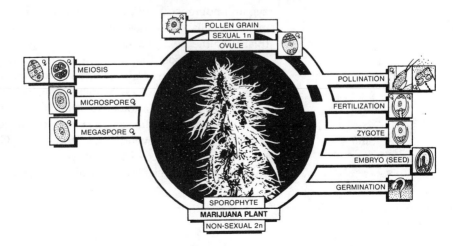

Alternation of generations involves the alternating of non-sexual (sporophytic — marijuana plant) and sexual (gametophytic — pollen grain, ovule) phases of the same organism. The seed contains the embryonic marijuana plant sporophyte. After germination the seedling marijuana sporophyte consists of the first bud and its stem, the epicotyl. Next, continuing downward, are the first leaves, the cotyledons. Below the cotyledons is the first stem unit, the hypocotyl, and the first root, the radicle (see Figure 3). The marijuana plant's sporophytic phase represents growth from the embryo to reproduction. The production of flowers begins sporogenesis and marks the maturation of the plant. During sporogenesis, the microspore mother cells undergo meiosis [a special type of nuclear division in which the diploid chromosome number (2n) is divided in half (haploid, 1n), and genetic segregation occurs]. This is followed by mitosis (the original chromosome number is preserved by replication, and segregation of genes does not usually occur), giving rise to the pollen grain (sperm), which is the male gametophyte (plant). The megaspore mother cells follow the same process, only they give rise to the ovule (egg), which is the female gametophyte (plant) and eventually becomes the seed.

The life cycle has now moved into the sexual phase of growth. Following pollination, the pollen tube attaches itself to the ovule (egg); the pollen tube bursts, releasing its sperm into the cytoplasm of the female gametophyte (plant). When the sperm and egg flow together, fertilization has occurred and the zygote — an individual developing from the union of two gametes (sperm and egg) — is produced. The zygote undergoes a series of nuclear cell divisions, forming a mass of cells. This mass of cells is the young sporophyte (plant) of the next generation. The young marijuana plant is nourished by food that was transported and stored by the parent plant. The embryo then becomes dormant after digesting most of the food, which is usually absorbed into the cotyledons. The embryonic sporophyte will remain in this dormant stage until the seed comes in contact with a suitable environment and eventually germinates. Germination is merely the emergence of the embryonic plant into the external environment; thus the life cycle is initiated again.

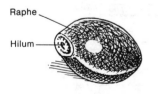

Raphe

Hilum

Figure 3.

Seeds

Seed Selection

Any type of marijuana seed yields good results with the water culture method. However, as mentioned earlier, there are tropical and temperate varieties of cannabis. A pure tropical strain from the state of Oaxaca, in southern Mexico, produces a good variety, well-suited to the water culture method. Oaxaca has a tropical wet-and-dry climate. Seventy-five percent of the rain falls between May and September. Occasional days of continuous rain occur in July and August, which is why the Oaxaca highlands receive some of the highest amounts of rain recorded in Mexico. This is followed by a prolonged dry season from October to May; these are the low-photoperiod months required for flowering. This wet-and-dry climate contributes to the quality of the plant (which will be discussed along with reproductive growth). The soil of the Oaxacan highlands is very fertile, with optimal mineral concentrations. As noted, Oaxaca is in the tropics, but its altitude keeps daytime temperatures in the upper 70s to mid-80s, with night temperatures averaging between the mid-70s and the lower 70s throughout the year. Rain may cool the mornings, but by mid-afternoon the temperature returns to the average. Because of the mineral content of the soil, the high moisture content of both soil and air, and the average temperatures, Oaxaca produces a very high-quality marijuana, which is ideal for controlled environmental growth with the water culture method.

Seed Storage

Seeds are best stored at low temperatures and low concentrations of oxygen. This keeps them viable longer by slowing down the rate of respiration. Ninety percent germination is easily obtained with relatively fresh seed. Seeds older than three to four years decline to less than twenty percent germination in general, and are therefore discarded. An airtight mason jar, kept in a refrigerator set at 45 degrees F, works fine for storage purposes.

Seed Germination

The environmental factors influencing germination are temperature, nutrients, atmosphere, and light.

Seeds can withstand a wide range of temperatures when dry, but only a very narrow range after germination. The optimal temperature for germination depends heavily on the variety of plant used. The only way to determine optimal temperatures for germination is to experiment with various temperature ranges and calculate the percentage of germination in each. When these experiments are performed, it is essential to keep the nutrients, atmosphere, and light the same for each temperature range.

High mineral concentration in contact with the seed may produce an osmotic effect that causes water to move from the seed into the nutrient solution, thereby preventing the seed from obtaining enough water. Again, if the radicle does not protrude from the seed coat, the tissues will dehydrate and die. For germination, a mixture of Dr. Chatelier should be one-half the dose given in the directions for hydroponic use.

The germinating embryos must be kept in a location that allows free gaseous exchange with the atmosphere. Oxygen is necessary for cell division to occur in the germinating embryo.

Marijuana seeds can germinate either in light or in darkness. However, it has been shown that although the radicle may emerge from the seed coat in total darkness, this occurs only in 15 to 20 percent of the germinating population, and further development of the embryo is still impossible without light. (Moreover, fungal growth rapidly overtakes the moist, warm, dark embryo tissues.) In contrast, when the germinating population is exposed to photoperiods of 18 hours per day, 85 to 95 percent of the embryos germinate and develop.

The best germinating medium is coarse vermiculite, which allows the maximum amount of oxygen to be drawn into the roots while nutrient solution is being added. Vermiculite is also easy to remove from the seedling roots before placing them in the growth tanks. The vermiculite is placed in a suitable container (e.g., a pie pan or cake pan), filling it to about 1/2" from the top. The nutrient solution is then mixed as described above, and used to gently fill the container around the sides until the solution can be seen just above the surface of the vermiculite. It is important that the hilum (a small pore at the end of the seed which is relatively permeable to water) be positioned at the surface of the vermiculite, with the raphe (a ridge or seam along the outside of the seed coat) facing downward (see Figure 4). This ensures maximum contact of the hilum with the nutrient solution and keeps the radicle extending down and not along the surface, where it would become photosynthetic and would be inhibited, or even prevented, from germinating further.

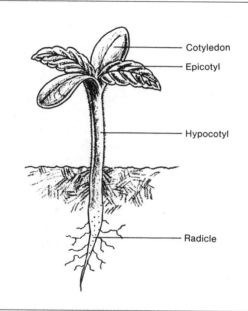

Figure 4.

The first phase of germination is the absorption of water. Dormant seeds contain about 20 percent water; actively growing seeds, 95 percent water. Hydration increases enzymatic activity, using stored food from the parent plant. The embryo eventually increases in size and cracks open the seed coat. The first part to emerge is the radicle. As the radicle pushes downward, the hypocotyl extends upward and becomes photosynthetic. The seed coat continues to cover the cotyledons for a short time, until the cotyledons have digested all of the stored food. They then enlarge, shedding the seed coat. After the cotyledons have emerged and the seedling is growing on its own, the nutrient solution of Dr.

Chatelier is increased to the full dose recommended for hydroponic use in the directions. The plants must be kept wet! At this point, solution is gently added around the plants to allow oxygen to be drawn into the medium. When the plants have reached a height of four to six inches, they are ready to be transplanted to the growth tanks. (See the section on assembly and operating procedures in the final chapter of this book.)

Vegetative Growth

As mentioned earlier, vegetative growth of the sporophyte occurs during the period between the emergence of the plant from seed to the onset of flowering. Development of the plant during this stage of the life cycle depends on cell division, cell enlargement, and cell differentiation.

Plant growth substances, termed phytohormones, are responsible for regulating such aspects of vegetative growth. There are three basic plant growth substances: (1) auxins, (2) gibberillins, and (3) cytokinins. The response of cannabis to plant growth substances in general has not been widely documented; however, it is well established that auxins inhibit branching.

In seed plants, branches originate from a dome-shaped mass of cells in the axils ("armpits") of leaves. The original structures are known as axillary or lateral buds. When the bud develops into a shoot, the apical meristem (actively growing tip) is slowly organized, usually duplicating the growth pattern found in the parent shoot tip. Auxins are produced in the apical meristem and then transported down the stem. If the source of auxin is removed by pruning the apical meristem, the branches are released from the auxin's inhibiting effects and undergo rapid development. Removal of the apical meristem is a method used by many horticulturists to encourage the increased production of floral buds.

This is particularly true, of course, in the case of marijuana.

When the apical meristem is removed, the development of two axillary buds in the leaf axils directly below is stimulated. Now the plant is developing two branches where it would have produced one — and each shoot is capable of producing floral buds.

Another advantage of removing the apical meristem is the promotion of horizontal growth, which allows the plant to remain shorter. This is a critical factor, especially in view of the low ceiling heights of some marijuana growth chambers (such as those in basement locations).

When the apical meristem is removed, the size and number of foliage leaves are reduced. However, even though this occurs, successful growers remove the foliage leaves (except for the two directly below the apical meristem) from the branch at the time when the apical meristem of the branch is removed. Although this method may seem odd at first, it has been well demonstrated that when foliage leaves reach full expansion there is a rapid decline in chlorophyll concentration and a decrease in the rate of photosynthesis. Through the removal of the less efficient foliage leaves, young leaves are allowed to expand quickly, increasing chlorophyll production and the rate of photosynthesis.

The foliage leaves are not discarded. They are collected and stored in an airtight container until the end of the plant's life cycle. (A method for extraction of their THC will be given in a later section.) Since a great deal of time and effort has gone into the production of each plant, growers utilize all parts of any value.

The leaves and apical meristems are removed once a week for five weeks after the plants have been placed in the growth tanks.

It has been mentioned in the literature that pruning the vegetative apical meristems before flowering will cause the plant to flower late or not to flower at all. (It was suggested that if the meristematic tissues responsible for sensing change were removed, the plant would no longer be able to determine when it was time to flower.) However, it has been established that the photoperiodic response is perceived by the leaves and not by the apical meristem. Further, it is a well-documented view that the flower and the vegetative shoots are not related structures, and that their meristems are basically different.

Floral induction is not a sudden change, but a series of stages. It has been found that when apical meristems are removed one week prior to the floral induction photoperiod, flowering is neither delayed nor prevented. Again, growers prune the apical meristems and the foliage leaves once a week, from the end of the first week to the beginning of the fifth week of growth. At the beginning of the sixth week, the floral induction photoperiod has started, and all pruning of the leaves and apical meristems is stopped for the duration of flowering.

Reproductive Growth

When the photoperiodic change is perceived by the leaves, the florigen (the flowering stimulus) is produced in the leaves and transported to the apical meristems where floral formation is initiated. The floral apical meristems replace the vegetative ones directly, usually by the development of inflorescence (an axis bearing flowers, or a flower cluster). With both sexes, the first evidence of flowering is seen in the formation of primordia (tiny shoots in the earliest stage of development) at a node (point of attachment of a leaf to a stem; also a branch emergence) of the principal stem adjacent to the axillary bud itself. Primordia are initially undifferentiated, but later males show their rounded form, with females showing enlargement of the single pointed bract (modified leaf — see Figure 5).

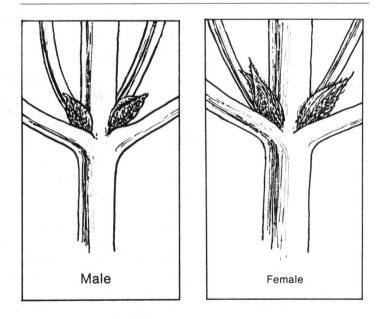

Male

Female

Figure 5.

Cannabis is considered a dioecious plant, meaning that the male and female flowers develop on separate plants. Monoecism (in which male and female flowers develop on the same plant) does occur, but can be controlled by changing the length of the photoperiod. (See the section on photoperiodism in Chapter 1.) This is important for pollination techniques (see Clarke). The most easily detected change from the vegetative to the reproductive phase in cannabis is the sudden increase in the elongation of the internodes (the region of the stem between two nodes). This is particularly true in male plants. Furthermore, the males are more copiously branched, and show speedier reduction of leaves into the form of floral bracts, with a reduction in relative chlorophyll content. Female plants, on the other hand, appear shorter and leafier than the males. All of these characteristics can be helpful in determining the sex of a plant; however, they are very general characteristics, and should by no means be considered absolute indicators of gender. Indeed, both male and female plants grown in an environmental growth chamber, and pruned on a weekly basis, appear short and bushy, so sex determination cannot be made until the early floral stages. Furthermore, physiological tests (such as respiratory rate, sap pH, and pigment content) have failed to reveal any differences in physiological characteristics between the two sexes. (For illustrations and descriptions of male and female flowers, see Figures 6 and 7.)

As noted in the description of female flowers, glandular trichomes (hairs) are associated with THC production. They contain very large amounts of resin, and the volume may be several times that of the excretory cells responsible for their production. Glandular trichomes are more abundant during the peak floral stage on the undersides of the leaves, and in the floral bracts and petioles. More are produced on female plants than on males, though they are quite numerous on the males as well. In fact, studies have shown that male plants possess as many cannabinoids per unit of fresh weight as do female plants with the same amount of flowering. However, after the male plant has shed its pollen, the flowers wither and die, which stops resin production, while the maturing female flowers continue to develop more copious amounts of resin-containing trichomes. Because of the

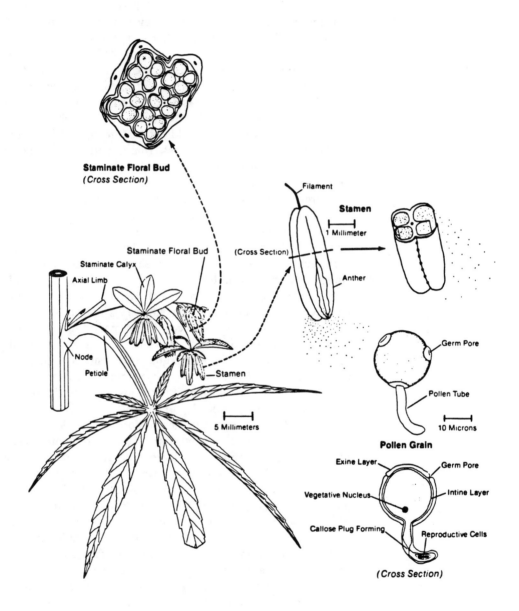

Figure 6.

In male flowers, five petals (approximately 5 millimeters, or 3/16" long) make up the calyx. They may be yellow, white, or green in color. They hang down, and five stamens (approximately 5 millimeters long) emerge, consisting of slender anthers (pollen sacs), splitting upwards from the tip and suspended on thin filaments. The exterior surface of the staminate calyx is covered with non-glandular trichomes. The pollen grains are nearly spherical, slightly yellow, and 25 to 30 microns (μ) in diameter. The surface is smooth and exhibits 2 to 4 germ pores. From *Marijuana Botany*, Clarke, (p. 49).

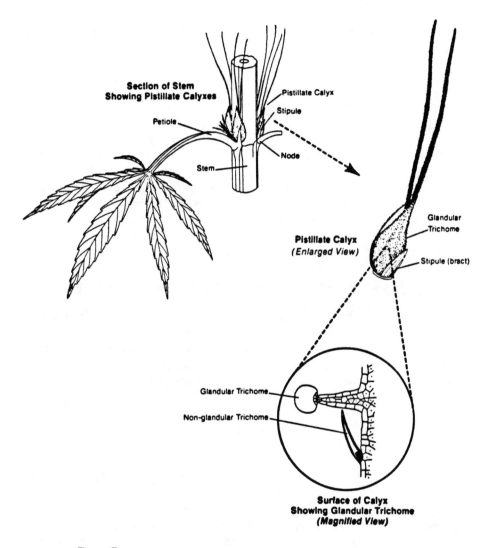

Figure 7.

The female flowers appear as two long white, yellow, or pink pistils protruding from the fold of a very thin membranous calyx. The calyx is covered with resin-exuding glandular trichomes (hairs). Pistillate flowers are borne in pairs at the nodes on each side of the petiole behind the stipule of bracts (reduced leaves) which conceal the flowers. The calyx measures 2 to 6 millimeters in length and is closely applied to, and completely contains, the ovary. From *Marijuana Botany*, Clarke, (p. 50).

high resin content of the male plants, their foliage leaves should be stripped and stored with the others for extraction of THC if the plants are not to be used for breeding purposes.

The exact function of the glandular trichomes and of the resins they contain is not well understood. One possibility is that the increased amount of resin produced during the peak floral stage of the female flowers functions as protective insulation of the delicate ovaries, and the subsequent seeds, against desiccation (drying) and insect predation.

It has been demonstrated, by controlling the relative humidity and the amount of water available to the roots for absorption, that there is a direct correlation between desiccation and the influence on THC production. After the female flowers have reached the two-week phase of development, the relative humidity of the growth chamber is dropped from the previously maintained level of 60–70 percent to zero, and the amount of solution in the growth tanks is reduced to half the amount previously available for absorption. The plants overall respond favorably by producing extremely plentiful, resin-filled trichomes. Also, this technique will in no way inhibit or prevent continued development of the female flowers. This does lend support to the notion that the glandular trichomes and their resins are related to an environmental response of desiccation.

Details on techniques of inducing desiccation deliberately, in order to enhance production of resins, will be given in the final chapter of this book.

Harvesting

The time of harvesting depends upon the variety of the plant used. Each type has a different rate of maturation. However, there is one general guideline that applies to all varieties of cannabis. Growers take accurate daily growth records of the length of the flowers. When elongation slows and stops, the flowers have usually reached maturity and glandular trichome production is at its peak. This is the time to remove the flowers from the plant. They are cut from the branch or stem below the two leaf nodes located directly beneath the flower. The nodes then provide a mechanism for hanging the flower during the curing process.

Curing

The purpose of the curing process is to allow the plant tissues to break down metabolically to yield the texture and aroma desired for smoking, which are strictly a matter of personal preference. There are many methods of curing; the method discussed here works well.

String or twine is attached to two points to form a "clothesline." On the string, the flower is hung upside down by the notch in the nodes. Hanging the flower upside down allows the leaves and floral bracts to surround the delicate resin-covered calyx, and protects it from handling damage. Curing is best done in low light or in darkness, and at humidity levels between 40 percent and 60 percent. However, fungi and bacteria thrive in this type of environment, and care must be taken to ensure that contamination of the flowers does not occur. If the area is disinfected thoroughly and a very slight flow of air maintained, no problems should arise. This method causes chlorophyll to become inactive (because of the paucity or absence of light), and the humidity prevents rapid drying of the floral tissues, thereby allowing chlorophyll and other plant metabolites to be broken down slowly. Clarke suggests that if curing of the tissues is done quickly, insufficient gaseous exchange with the intercellular tissues occurs; this causes the "greenness" to be locked in, and no amount of further curing will remove it. This has generally been found to be true. The more slowly the tissues can be cured, the milder the taste. A moister texture also results.

Extraction

Since so much time, labor, and cost has gone into the production of each plant, growers do not overlook utilization of the "shake" or leaves. Extraction involves the process of removing the essential oil, THC, from the leaves remaining on the plant and those removed during pruning. This is accomplished through the use of a solvent in which the oil will dissolve, which is later separated from the plant material by passing it through an appropriate filter.

The best solvent found to date is chloroform. It is non-flammable, which makes it safer to handle than ethanol. Further, it has a low boiling point (61 degrees C), and a residue after evaporation of .0005 percent. The low residue percentage means that virtually no trace solvent remains to contaminate the oil and cause an aftertaste, which is usually a problem encountered with ethanol unless time-consuming distillation processes are used. Another important concern is that chlorophyll is relatively insoluble in chloroform, eliminating the heavy "green" taste that always results from ethanol extractions.

To initiate the extraction process, the leaves must be dried thoroughly. This can be done by placing them on fairly absorbent paper, such as newsprint, in a good sunny spot near a window. (Fresh newsprint paper may be obtained in most art supply stores. The lead content of ordinary newspapers makes them unsuitable for this purpose.) The leaves are then turned over every few days to ensure complete drying. When they are sufficiently dry, the leaves should be brittle and crumble easily between the fingers. When the leaves have completely dried, they are placed in a blender and ground to a fine powder. Studies have shown that to achieve 90 percent extraction of the oil, the plant material must be powdered. This is because nearly as much oil is contained in non-glandular internal tissues as is produced by the glandular trichomes.

Next, a filter (the type used for automatic coffee makers) is placed over a clean Pyrex beaker or Corning Ware dish. The plant material is piled about halfway to the top of the filter, and the rest of the material saved (if necessary) in an airtight plastic container. At this point, approximately 200 milliliters of chloroform are poured into the blender and sloshed around on the sides. This rinses out any oil remaining in the blender. Chloroform is poured from the blender over the plant material until it reaches the top of the filter (adding more chloroform if needed). When the chloroform has completely filtered into the beaker or dish, this process is then repeated by adding chloroform until it reaches the top of the filter. Two extractions of the same plant material are usually sufficient to remove all of its oil.

At this point, the plant material is discarded; the same procedure is repeated until the beaker or dish becomes full of solvent. Now the beaker or dish is placed on an electric stove or hot plate and heated slowly to a very low boil. When chloroform is being evaporated, the area must be completely ventilated! In the early days of medicine, chloroform was used as an anesthetic until harmful side effects (such as liver damage) were discovered, so it is clear that extreme care must be used when evaporating this solvent. After the solvent has been removed, the same procedure is repeated until all of the plant material has been treated. The oil is collected and stored in a pipette (small glass tube). These can be obtained at any scientific supply company and are inexpensive. The oil is drawn into the tube (this may be easier if the oil is first heated a bit), and the tube capped at both ends. The storage procedure is the same as that outlined for floral tops.

Storage

After the flowers have been cured to the desired extent, they are stored to prevent further drying and breakdown of the floral tissues. This can be accomplished by one of two methods. The first is to store the flowers in a mason jar or similar container, which can be sealed and kept airtight. The jar or container is maintained in an environment of low light and humidity. Once the oxygen in the container has been used for the further metabolic breakdown of tissues, drying will cease.

Another alternative is to use a small vacuum food processing unit. This is probably the most efficient way to store the flowers. By placing a vacuum pump on the container (again an airtight one), with the flowers inside the container, and sealing tightly, further curing is eliminated instantly by removing all oxygen with the vacuum. The advantage of this method is that it gives plant tissues an essentially unlimited shelf life: they will last for years. Growers generally check with sellers of food processors and laboratory equipment for systems that can handle this particular method. As with the first method, the final product is stored in low light and humidity.

Growth Data

Growth can be measured in various ways. For most applications, height and width measurements of the plant are all that is necessary. However, individual leaf size (length, width, and area); fresh and dry weight of particular organs, such as roots, stems, and leaves; and concentrations of chemical components (nucleic acids, soluble nitrogen, protein nitrogen, lipids and carbohydrates) are examples of other types of growth data that may be useful.

Growth Curves

Growth curves show an early period when the increase in size is very slow. This is followed by a period of rapid increase in size (height, dry weight, etc.). Next comes a third period, one of decreasing growth rate. The physiological processes of the three periods can be characterized as follows: (1) The early plant growth period is limited by food reserves in the seed. (2) When the seedling emerges and develops an adequate root system and enlarged leaf surface to support vigorous photosynthesis, a period of rapid increase in size usually occurs. (3) High metabolic rates cannot be maintained indefinitely, and cessation of growth results. The factors involved in decreasing growth are not well understood, but competition for essential metabolites, growth substances, water, and light — and, in addition, the accumulation of inhibitors, toxic substances, and waste materials — are all certainly contributing factors.

By keeping accurate growth data on height, girth, and dry weight, and plotting these against the time from germination, a sigmoid (S-shaped) growth curve (as shown in Figure 8) is obtained. As illustrated in the figure, the growth curve lends itself to mathematical manipulation. The rate of growth for height, shown at (A) and (B), is obtained by ruling a straight line tangent to the growth curve and constructing a right traingle with the tangent as hypotenuse. In the example shown, the horizontal leg of each triangle is drawn to equal 10 days; the vertical leg is then a measurement of the size increase during the 10-day period. The growth rate at (A) is then calculated to be 0.17 centimeters per day, while at (B) the rate is 0.75 centimeters per day.

Data of this kind are very valuable. It was discovered with a particular group of plants that, had accurate growth data been taken and had the plotting of growth curves been carried out, slowing growth could have been detected weeks before it became physically visible. These data could have led to corrective action, preventing irreversible damage to plant tissues and ultimate death.

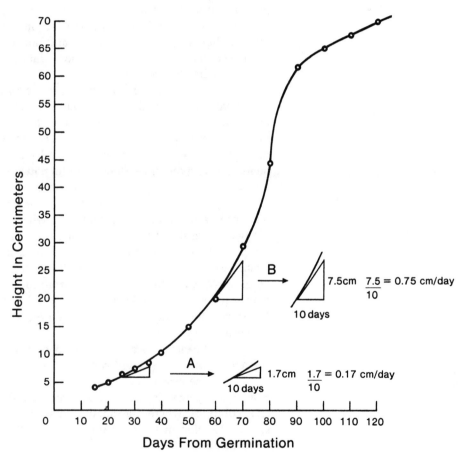

Figure 8.
Growth chart.

Computer Programs

As mentioned in the Preface to this book, computers are playing an ever-increasing role in the handling of human affairs. This is as true in the field of environmental plant growth as in any other field of human endeavor. Computers can maintain all the instruments that gather growth data, and can process the data into useful information. Computers with real-time capabilities, recording events as they occur in the real world, will be able to collect information from thermocouples to record room and solution temperatures, humidity from hygrometers, and CO_2 concentrations from gas analyzers, as well as controlling the timing sequences for the lights, fans, humidifiers, and air conditioners. Moreover, they can store and retrieve data pertaining to other growth processes.

Shown on the next few pages are two programs that have proven reliable in this kind of work. The first program was written to determine the net rate of photosynthesis so that the optimal CO_2 concentration in the growth chamber could be calculated, thereby increasing carbohydrate (food) production for the plant. The second is for the monitoring of general growth data.

(Note: In the general environmental growth data program, in line statement 380, when establishing the two-dimensional array, the second number enclosed in the parentheses is the number of days for which the user wishes to collect data. The number 5 was used strictly as an example. Since the average time from the placement of plants in the growth tanks to harvesting is between 11 and 12 weeks, the array should have a time dimension of between 77 and 84 days.)

An array is a special kind of variable. It can stand for numbers or strings (words).

The best way to think of a 2-dimensional array is as a box containing smaller squares, arranged in rows and columns, where information may be stored in a specific location in the computer memory, then retrieved for further use.

	Column #1	Column #2	Column #3
Row #1	A(1,1)	A(1,2)	A(1,3)
Row #2	A(2,1)	A(2,2)	A(2,3)
Row #3	A(3,1)	A(3,2)	A(3,3)

A(1,1), etc., represent locations in the computer's memory.

Since all computer systems have different read-write command statements that link the computer with peripheral devices, the listings given here are only the general programs and a sample of what each program states and asks when it is run on a computer, in order to illustrate the applications possible for computers in the controlled environmental growth of plants. These programs are written in a language called Digital BASIC Plus II, so they would most likely have to be altered somewhat if they were used in a specific system.

This program was designed to give an estimate of the amount of plant materials produced during photosynthesis. If these data are computed weekly throughout the vegetative phase of growth, there should be an increase in the NRP (net rate of photosynthesis). By correlating this information between generations of the same variety, or between different varieties, and by altering environmental influences, optimal rates of photosynthesis can be established.

```
9 PRINT
10 PRINT "              NET ASSIMILATION RATE"
11 PRINT
12 PRINT
13 PRINT
14 PRINT
15 PRINT
20 PRINT " THIS PROGRAM IS DESIGNED TO GIVE AN ESTIMATE OF
25 PRINT " THE NET RATE OF PHOTOSYNTHESIS"
27 PRINT
29 PRINT
30 PRINT " NAR IS DETERMINED BY CALCULATING THE DRY "
40 PRINT " WEIGHT ( ROOTS AND SHOOT LEAVES ) AND THE "
45 PRINT " SHOOT LEAVES SURFACE AREA DURING GROWTH "
47 PRINT
50 PRINT " THIS WILL GIVE THE AMOUNT OF PHOTOSYNTHETIC "
55 PRINT " PRODUCT GOING TO PLANT MATERIAL"
57 PRINT
59 PRINT
60 PRINT " ( W(C)-W(I) ) * 2.303 * ( LOG(10) A(C)-LOG(10) A(I) )"
70 PRINT " NAR= ----------------------------------------"
80 PRINT "              ( T(C)-T(O) ) * ( A(C)-A(I) )"
85 PRINT
87 PRINT
90 PRINT " TAKE EQUAL AMOUNTS OF PLANT MATERIAL (ROOTS"
95 PRINT " AND SHOOT LEAVES ) AND BE SURE THERE IS A "
100 PRINT " SUFFICIENT AMOUNT TO CALCULATE THE DRY "
105 PRINT " WEIGHT IN GRAMS"
107 PRINT
110 PRINT " BEFORE DRYING THE SHOOT LEAVES, DETERMINE THE "
115 PRINT " SHOOT LEAVES SURFACE AREA IN SQUARE
117 PRINT " CENTIMETERS"
119 PRINT
120 PRINT " DO YOU WISH TO CONTINUE WITH THIS PROGRAM: 1) YES "
125 PRINT "                                            2) NO "
130 INPUT V
135 IF V= 1 THEN 150
140 IF V= 2 THEN 530
145 PRINT
147 PRINT
150 PRINT " W(I)= THE INITIAL DRY WEIGHT OF ROOTS AND
155 PRINT " SHOOT LEAVES"
157 PRINT
160 PRINT " IS THIS PREVIOUSLY ENTERED DATA: 1) YES"
165 PRINT "                                  2) NO"
167 INPUT W
170 IF W= 1 THEN 210
180 IF W= 2 THEN 190
185 PRINT
187 PRINT
190 PRINT " WHAT IS THE INITIAL DRY WEIGHT OF THE ROOTS
195 PRINT " AND SHOOT LEAVES IN GRAMS"
197 PRINT
200 INPUT A
205 PRINT
207 PRINT
210 PRINT " W(C)= THE CURRENT WEEKLY DRY WEIGHT OF THE
215 PRINT " ROOTS AND SHOOT LEAVES"
```

```
217 PRINT
219 PRINT
220 PRINT " WHAT IS THE CURRENT DRY WEIGHT OF THE ROOTS AND
225 PRINT " SHOOT LEAVES IN GRAMS"
227 PRINT
230 INPUT B
235 PRINT
237 PRINT
240 PRINT " A(I)= THE INITIAL AREA OF THE SHOOT LEAVES IN
245 PRINT " SQUARE CENTIMETERS"
247 PRINT
248 PRINT
250 PRINT " IS THIS PREVIOUSLY ENTERED DATA: 1) YES"
255 PRINT "                                    2) NO"
257 PRINT
260 INPUT X
265 IF X= 1 THEN 300
270 IF X= 2 THEN 280
275 PRINT
277 PRINT
280 PRINT " WHAT IS THE INITIAL AREA OF THE SHOOT LEAVES IN
285 PRINT " SQUARE CENTIMETERS"
287 PRINT
290 INPUT C
295 PRINT
297 PRINT
300 PRINT " A(C)= THE CURRENT WEEKLY AREA OF THE SHOOT
305 PRINT " LEAVES IN SQUARE CENTIMETERS"
307 PRINT
310 PRINT " WHAT IS THE CURRENT AREA OF THE SHOOT LEAVES IN
315 PRINT " SQUARE CENTIMETERS"
317 PRINT
320 INPUT D
325 PRINT
327 PRINT
330 PRINT " T(O)= THE INITIAL TIME IN WHICH THE PLANTS WERE
335 PRINT " PLACED IN THE GROWTH TANKS"
340 PRINT " IS THIS PREVIOUSLY ENTERED DATA: 1) YES"
345 PRINT "                                    2) NO"
347 PRINT
350 INPUT Y
355 IF Y= 1 THEN 390
360 IF Y= 2 THEN 370
370 PRINT " ENTER ZERO"
375 PRINT
380 INPUT E
385 PRINT
387 PRINT
390 PRINT " T(C)= THE CURRENT NUMBER OF WEEKS SINCE THE
395 PRINT " PLANTS WERE PLACED IN THE GROWTH TANKS"
397 PRINT
399 PRINT
400 PRINT " HOW MANY WEEKS HAVE THE PLANTS BEEN IN THE GROWTH TANKS "
405 PRINT
410 INPUT F
```

```
415 PRINT
417 PRINT
420   R=((B-A*2.303*((LOG(D)/LOG(10))-
          (LOG(C)/LOG(10))))/((F-E)*(D-C))
425 PRINT
430 PRINT "NAR=";R
435 PRINT
437 PRINT
440 PRINT " DO YOU WISH TO:   1) RUN NAR PROGRAM AGAIN"
450 PRINT
455 PRINT "                   2) REENTER DATA"
457 PRINT
460 PRINT "                   3) STOP"
470 INPUT Z
480 IF Z < 1 THEN 440
490 IF Z > 3 THEN 440
500 IF Z = 1 THEN 420
510 IF Z = 2 THEN 150
520 IF Z = 3 THEN 530
530 END
```

The following is a sample of output from the program given above. The numbers given in boldface are those typed in by the user after receiving the "?" prompt.

```
                    NET ASSIMILATION RATE

THIS PROGRAM IS DESIGNED TO GIVE AN ESTIMATE OF THE NET
            RATE OF PHOTOSYNTHESIS

NAR IS DETERMINED BY CALCULATING THE DRY WEIGHT ( ROOTS
            AND SHOOT LEAVES ) AND THE SHOOT LEAVES SURFACE
            AREA   DURING GROWTH

THIS WILL GIVE THE AMOUNT OF PHOTOSYNTHETIC PRODUCT GOING
            TO PLANT MATERIAL

      (W(C)-W(I) ) * 2.303 * ( LOG(10) A(C)-LOG(10) A(I) )"
NAR= -------------------------------------------------"
              ( T(C)-T(O) ) * ( A(C)-A(I) )"

TAKE EQUAL AMOUNTS OF PLANT MATERIAL (ROOTS AND SHOOT
            LEAVES) AND BE SURE THERE IS A SUFFICIENT AMOUNT
            TO CALCULATE THE DRY WEIGHT IN GRAMS

BEFORE DRYING THE SHOOT LEAVES, DETERMINE THE SHOOT LEAVES
            SURFACE AREA IN SQUARE CENTIMETERS

DO YOU WISH TO CONTINUE WITH THIS PROGRAM: 1) YES    2) NO

? 1
W(I)= THE INITIAL DRY WEIGHT OF ROOTS AND SHOOT LEAVES

IS THIS PREVIOUSLY ENTERED DATA: 1) YES          2) NO
```

? **2**

WHAT IS THE INITIAL DRY WEIGHT OF THE ROOTS AND SHOOT LEAVES IN
　　　　GRAMS

? **2**

W(C)= THE CURRENT WEEKLY DRY WEIGHT OF THE ROOTS AND SHOOT
　　　　LEAVES

WHAT IS THE CURRENT DRY WEIGHT OF THE ROOTS AND SHOOT LEAVES IN
　　　　GRAMS

? **4**

A(I)= THE INITIAL AREA OF THE SHOOT LEAVES IN SQUARE
　　　　CENTIMETERS

IS THIS PREVIOUSLY ENTERED DATA: 1) YES　　　　　　　2) NO

? **2**

WHAT IS THE INITIAL AREA OF THE SHOOT LEAVES IN SQUARE
　　　　CENTIMETERS

? **8**

T(O)= THE INITIAL TIME IN WHICH THE PLANTS WERE PLACED IN THE
　　　　GROWTH TANKS

IS THIS PREVIOUSLY ENTERED DATA: 1) YES　　　　　　　2) NO

? **2**

ENTER ZERO

? **0**

T(C)= THE CURRENT NUMBER OF WEEKS SINCE THE PLANTS WERE PLACED
　　　　IN THE GROWTH TANKS

HOW MANY WEEKS HAVE THE PLANTS BEEN IN THE GROWTH TANKS

? **2**

NAR= .173318

DO YOU WISH TO:　　　　1) RUN NAR PROGRAM AGAIN

　　　　　　　　　　2) REENTER DATA

　　　　　　　　　　3) STOP

The program that follows was written to keep a daily record of the various types of environmental growth data. Again, this information is very important. Should a crop of plants run into trouble, this type of data can aid in early detection.

```
010 PRINT              "ENVIRONMENTAL GROWTH DATA"
020 PRINT
030 PRINT
040 PRINT
050 PRINT "THIS PROGRAM DETERMINES THE ENVIRONMENTAL GROWTH  DAT"
060 PRINT "DO YOU WISH TO CONTINUE: YES OR NO"
070 INPUT X$
075 PRINT
077 PRINT
080 IF X$ = "Y" THEN 120
090 IF X$ = "N" THEN 600
095 IF X$ <> "N" GO TO 060
100 PRINT
110 PRINT
120 PRINT "THE PROGRAM WILL LIST THE DAY NUMBER, FOLLOWED   "
130 PRINT "BY THE ENVIRONMENTAL DATA REQUIRED BELOW."
140 PRINT
145 PRINT
150 PRINT
155 PRINT
160 PRINT "LIST OF ENVIRONMENTAL DATA REQUIRED:"
170 PRINT
175 PRINT
180 PRINT "CHAMBER TEMPERATURE => TEMPERATURE OF CHAMBER    "
190 PRINT TAB (24);"IN DEGREES CENTIGRADE"
200 PRINT
210 PRINT "SOLUTION TEMPERATURE => TEMPERATURE OF SOLUTION  "
220 PRINT TAB (24);"IN DEGREES CENTIGRADE"
230 PRINT
240 PRINT "RELATIVE HUMIDITY => PERCENTAGE PRESENT IN THE"
250 PRINT TAB (24);"CHAMBER ATMOSPHERE"
260 PRINT
270 PRINT "CARBON DIOXIDE => NUMBER OF POUNDS OF PRESSURE"
280 PRINT TAB (24);"REMAINING IN THE CYLINDER"
290 PRINT
300 PRINT "HEIGHT => HEIGHT OF THE PLANT GIVEN IN"
305 PRINT TAB (24);"CENTIMETERS"
310 PRINT
320 PRINT "GIRTH ( WIDTH ) => MEASURED ACROSS THE WIDTH OF   "
330 PRINT TAB (24);"THE PLANT FROM LEAF TIP TO LEAF TIP,    "
340 PRINT TAB (24);"GIVEN IN CENTIMETERS"
350 PRINT
360 PRINT
370 PRINT
380 DIM A(12,5)
390 FOR J = 1 TO 5
```

```
400 FOR J = 1 TO 12
410 IF I = 1 THEN A$ = "DAY"
420 IF I = 1 THEN W$ = "CHAMBER TEMPERATURE"
430 IF I = 2 THEN W$ = "SOLUTION TEMPERATURE"
440 IF I = 3 THEN W$ = "RELATIVE HUMIDITY"
450 IF I = 4 THEN W$ = "CARBON DIOXIDE"
460 IF I = 5 THEN W$ = "PLANT #1 : HEIGHT"
470 IF I = 6 THEN W$ = "PLANT #1 : GIRTH"
480 IF I = 7 THEN W$ = "PLANT #2 : HEIGHT"
490 IF I = 8 THEN W$ = "PLANT #2 : GIRTH"
500 IF I = 9 THEN W$ = "PLANT #3 : HEIGHT"
510 IF I = 10 THEN W$ = "PLANT #3 : GIRTH"
520 IF I = 11 THEN W$ = "PLANT #4 : HEIGHT"
530 IF I = 12 THEN W$ = "PLANT #4 : GIRTH"
540 PRINT A$;"....";J
550 PRINT "INPUT DATA....";W$

560 INPUT A(I,J)
570 PRINT
580 NEXT I
590 NEXT J
600 END
```

Again, the following is sample output from the program given above, with the user's input (which is entered at the "?" prompt) shown in boldface.

```
ENVIRONMENTAL GROWTH DATA


THIS PROGRAM DETERMINES THE ENVIRONMENTAL GROWTH DATA. DO YOU
                      WISH TO CONTINUE: YES OR NO
? Y

THE PROGRAM WILL LIST THE DAY NUMBER, FOLLOWED BY THE
                      ENVIRONMENTAL DATA REQUIRED BELOW

LIST OF ENVIRONMENTAL DATA REQUIRED:

CHAMBER TEMPERATURE  => TEMPERATURE OF CHAMBER IN DEGREES
                        CENTIGRADE

SOLUTION TEMPERATURE => TEMPERATURE OF SOLUTION IN DEGREES
                        CENTIGRADE

RELATIVE HUMIDITY    => PERCENTAGE PRESENT IN THE CHAMBER
                        ATMOSPHERE

CARBON DIOXIDE       => NUMBER OF POUNDS OF PRESSURE REMAINING
                        IN THE CYLINDER

HEIGHT               => HEIGHT OF THE PLANT GIVEN IN
                        CENTIMETERS
```

```
GIRTH ( WIDTH )      => MEASURED ACROSS THE WIDTH OF THE
                        PLANT FROM LEAF TIP TO LEAF
                        TIP, GIVEN IN CENTIMETERS


DAY.... 1
INPUT DATA....CHAMBER TEMPERATURE
? 90

DAY....1
INPUT DATA....SOLUTION TEMPERATURE
? 86

DAY....1
INPUT DATA....RELATIVE HUMIDITY
? 60

DAY.... 1
INPUT DATA....CARBON DIOXIDE
? 1000

DAY....1
INPUT DATA....PLANT #1 : HEIGHT
? 34

DAY....1
INPUT DATA....PLANT #1 : GIRTH
? 56

DAY....1
INPUT DATA....PLANT #2 : HEIGHT
? 33

DAY....1
INPUT DATA....PLANT #2 : GIRTH
? 57

DAY....1
INPUT DATA....PLANT #3 : HEIGHT
? 32

DAY....1
INPUT DATA....PLANT #3 : GIRTH
? 59

DAY....1
INPUT DATA....PLANT #4 : HEIGHT
? 33

DAY....1
INPUT DATA....PLANT #4 : GIRTH
? 59

DAY.... 2
INPUT DATA....CHAMBER TEMPERATURE
?
```

References

Adams, R., D. C. Pease and J. H. Clark. 1940. Isolation of Cannabidiol and quebrachitol from red oil of Minnesota wild hemp. *Journal of the American Chemical Society* 62: 2194.

Blackman, G. E. 1961. Responses to environmental factors by plants in the vegetative phase. Pages 525–556 in M. X. Zarrow, ed. *Growth in Living Systems*. Basic Books, Inc., Publishers, NY.

Carr, D. J. 1967. The relationship between florigen and flowering hormones. *Annual New York Academy of Science* 144: 305–312.

*Clarke, R. C. 1981. *Marijuana Botany*. And/Or Press, Inc., Berkeley, CA.

Dayanandau, D. and P. B. Kaufman. 1976. Trichomes of Cannabis Sativa L. *American Journal of Botany* 63 (5): 578–597.

Esau, K. 1953. *Plant Anatomy*. John Wiley & Son, NY.

Fairbairn, J. W., J. A. Liebman and S. Simic. 1971. The tetra-hydro-cannabinol content of Cannabis leaf. *Journal of Pharmacy and Pharmacology* 23: 558–59.

Fairbairn, J. W. 1972. The trichomes and glands of Cannabis Sativa L. *Bulletin on Narcotics* 24 (4): 29–33.

Fairbairn, J. W. and J. A. Liebman. 1973. The extraction and estimation of the cannabinoids in Cannabis Sativa L. and its products. *Journal of Pharmaceutical Pharmacology* 25: 150–155.

Hammond, C. T. and P. G. Mahlberg. 1977. Morphogenesis of capitate glandular hairs of Cannabis Sativa. *American Journal of Botany* 64 (8): 1023–31.

Heslop-Harrison, J. and Y. Heslop-Harrison. 1969. Cannabis Sativa L. in Evans, L. T., *The Induction of Flowering*. Cornell University Press, Ithaca, NY.

Leopold, A. C. and P. E. Kriedemann. 1975. *Plant Growth and Development*, 2nd ed. McGraw-Hill Book Company, NY.

Sachs, R. M. and W. P. Hackett. 1969. Control of vegetative and reproductive development in seed plants. *Horticulture Science* 4: 103–107.

Salisbury, F. B. 1963. *The Flowering Process*. Pergamon Press, Inc., Elmsford, NY.

Plate 1. Plant one week after being placed in the growth tank.

Plate 2. Plants on right four weeks after placement in the growth tanks. Plants on left three weeks in the growth tanks.

Plate 3. Plants seven weeks after being placed in the growth tanks and one week after the floral induction photoperiod was initiated.

Plate 4. "Female" flowers of plant seven weeks after placement in the growth tanks and one week after the floral induction photoperiod was initiated.

Plate 5. "Female" flowers of plant nine weeks after placement in the growth tanks and three weeks after the floral induction photoperiod was initiated.

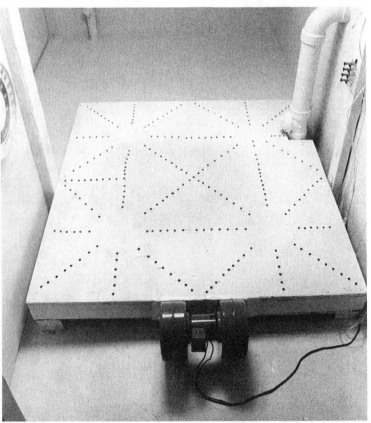

Plate 6. Air circulation platform. Note location of the air circulation holes. This allows for complete circulation of air around the entire circumference of the plants.

Plate 7. Multiple air valve. Make sure that it has the same number of air valves as growth tanks in the system.

Plate 9. ³/₈" hole as close to the bottom of the growth tanks as possible.

Plate 8. Float valve.

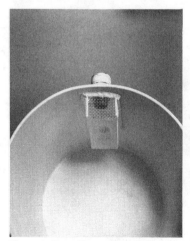

Plate 10. Run silicone around the edge of the screen and place the box over the threaded male hose couplings on the inside of the growth tanks.

Plate 11. Hold the backside of the male threaded couplings firmly with a pair of pliers, and screw on the seal caps tightly.

Plate 12. Completed growth tank.

Plate 13. ⁵/₈" diameter hole in the center and four inches from one end of the lid.

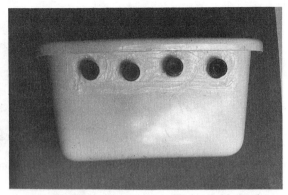

Plate 14. Front view of the constant level tank. Notice that white silicone is applied around the threaded couplings for protective purposes.

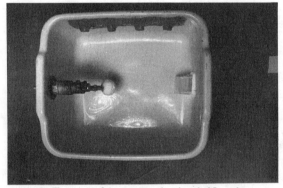

Plate 15. Top vew of the constant level tank. Note that silicone is applied around the threaded couplings for protective purposes.

Plate 16. Completed constant level tank and lid.

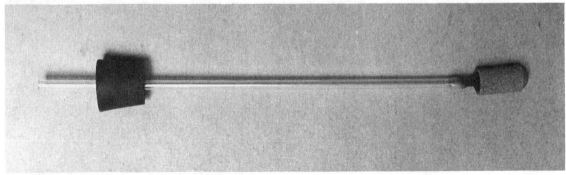

Plate 17. Completed aeration tube for the growth tanks.

Plate 18. Cradle for a round nutrient solution reservoir tank.

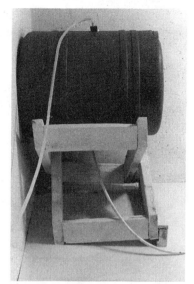

Plate 19. Completed nutrient solution reservoir tank in cradle.

Plate 20. Male threaded hose couplings on the growth tanks facing the constant level tank.

Plate 21. The water pump inlet hose with foot valve attached to the constant level tank.

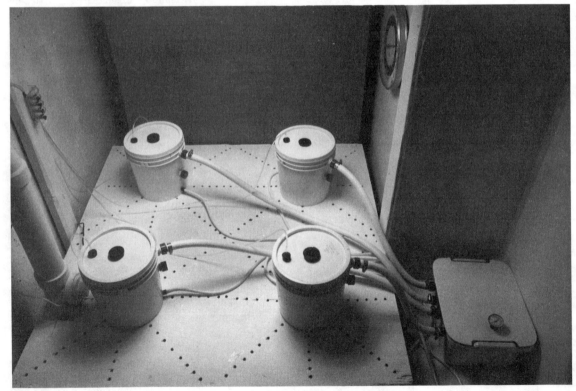

Plate 22. The water culture and aeration system completely assembled and circulating.

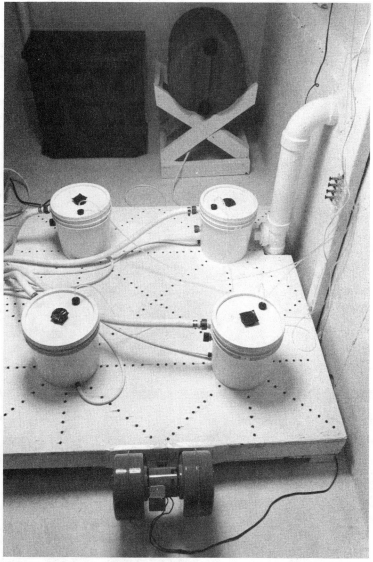

Plate 23. Completed environmental growth system.

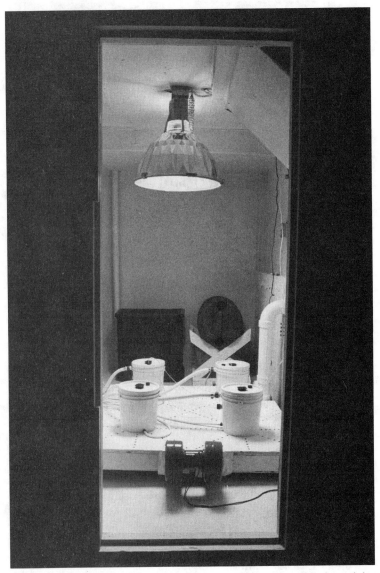

Plate 24. Completed environmental growth systems. The air conditioning unit is mounted in the wall to the left and is out of view.

6

Environmental Growth Systems Assimilation

A nuts-and-bolts look at the way marijuana is actually grown indoors. This chapter gives a step-by-step description of the construction of a growth chamber, including a list of all the parts and procedures required. It also provides all the necessary information on air circulation systems, carbon dioxide enrichment systems, and humidity control systems, all of which directly influence plant growth.

Growth Chamber

As the quality of artificial lighting has increased, growth chambers have become prominent in plant physiology experimentation. This has allowed researchers to investigate every aspect of environmental factors related to plant growth. Growth chambers are ideal for Cannabis research because, in addition to allowing complete environmental control, they also provide the privacy that is currently necessary for growing marijuana.

The most efficient location for a growth chamber is a basement or cellar. This provides the most constant temperature in and around the growth chamber. There is one potential disadvantage to the basement location: in general, basement ceilings are only eight feet in height. If the plants can be kept cut back, as discussed in Chapter 5, this is really not much of a problem. A ceiling height of less than six feet is not practical under any circumstances, though.

Bedrooms and closets whose walls are in contact with the outside of the house are less desirable as growth chambers, because they are exposed to constant variations in temperature. Large closets whose walls do not touch the outer walls work very well. Attics are used only as a last resort; it is almost certain that some means of heating and cooling will have to be used.

The size of the growth chamber is limited only by the amount of space available and the amount of money a grower is willing to invest. However, a few requirements should be kept in mind. Each plant needs at least four square feet of area, and the more the better. There should be two feet of access space on at least three sides of the whole area. An area of approximately 20 square feet is sufficient for the equipment and materials.

Presented here will be the construction of a growth chamber in a basement location. When laying out such a chamber, it is best to use one corner of the basement, with a drain nearby. This reduces the number of walls that must be constructed. For those who are unfamiliar with carpentry, there are many books on the design and construction of walls with window frames and doors. While roughing in the walls, a window frame the same size as an air conditioner should be constructed (see next section). This window frame must be positioned so that when the air conditioner is installed it will not blow air directly onto the plants.

Once the walls, door(s), and window frame have been constructed, wiring for at least three electrical outlets and for the light is installed. For safety considerations, all wiring should be done by a licensed professional electrician. However, a few points about wiring the light are valuable to keep in mind when talking with the electrician. The 1,000-watt Lucalox is designed so that the ballast and the fixture can be separated. This allows for the ballast to be placed outside of the growth chamber to prevent excessive heat. It is best to have the light on its own circuit breaker; this keeps the circuit from overloading and shutting down as a result of other household use of electricity.

The interior sides of the walls and ceiling are now ready to be sheet-rocked. (Sheet-rocking the outsides of the walls is optional; it is not really necessary.) It is easier, when sheet-rocking, first to nail the sheet-rock to the studs and then to cut the holes for the electrical outlets, door(s), window frame, and light. Two holes must also be drilled at the bottom of one wall for the inlet and outlet hoses of the water pump. This will allow the water pump to be placed outside of the growth chamber. Another hole must be drilled at the bottom of one wall so that a hose from the carbon dioxide cylinder may be run to the air circulation platform inside the chamber. All mating joints between the ceiling, walls, and floor, and any gaps or spaces connecting the chamber environment with the outside atmosphere, should be sealed with a silicone sealant.

Now the walls, ceiling, floor, and door(s) are ready to be painted with a flat or semigloss latex white paint. Aluminum foil is not as efficient as a white painted surface. The light it reflects is directional, meaning that some areas of the room will have higher light intensities than others. Also, all reflected heat places an increased stress on the air conditioner, and the amount of heat retained by the room to keep the proper temperature during the night break between lighting periods is questionable.

A white painted surface has virtually the same reflectivity, while diffusing the light and giving an overall evenness in light intensity throughout the room. The concrete and sheet-rock on which the white surface is applied will act as a heat sink, allowing the air conditioner to work less, and will then radiate off the heat absorbed during the night break to maintain the proper room temperature.

At this point the light should be installed in the growth room by the electrician. Be sure and ask the electrician to solder the light connection, and that it is well insulated to ensure that no shorts in the circuit will occur. An eye hook is then positioned in the ceiling directly above the light. A link chain, with one end attached to the fixture and the other end connected to the hook, will prevent any damage if the light accidentally falls.

Next, a hole is cut in the door. It should be the same size as an air ventilation grill (the type found in the walls of most homes). The grill is attached to the door two feet from the floor on the interior side. Then, on the outer side of the door, a piece of air conditioning filter is attached over the grill. (Silicone sealant works best.) If the room is sealed well, this grill provides a filtered source of air for the growth chamber, preventing pollen or other contaminants from entering.

When all these steps have been completed, the growth chamber is ready to be assembled with the air circulation system, as described in the section which follows.

Air Circulation System

Circulating air over the plants provides for the exchange of gases and reduces the temperature of the leaves. It is best to introduce the air from below the plants. In this way, heat that is given off by the leaves and the light is driven in the direction of its natural flow. Moreover, there is greater exposure of the plants to carbon dioxide; remember, the number of stomates is greater on the underside of a leaf than on its top. For supplying air circulation from below, a thin, airtight platform is used. Air is forced into the platform by means of a ventilation blower, and moves upward through holes in the top.

First, the type and size of the ventilation blower must be determined. The best kind of blower is the "squirrel cage" type. These blowers are commonly used for various heating and cooling systems, and are capable of delivering the high volumes of air required. Ideally, the entire volume of air contained by the platform should be changed once per second. Blowers are rated by the number of cubic feet of air they can deliver in one minute. For example, if the platform has a volume of four cubic feet, a blower that delivers 240 cubic feet per minute is required to change the air in the platform completely once per second.

In designing the platform, four square feet per plant is the absolute minimum area that must be allowed. If the platform is placed in a basement, the platform's height should be six inches or less, because of the low ceilings common in basements.

After these considerations have been taken into account, the frame of the platform is constructed. When the frame is complete, a sheet of 1/2" plywood is nailed over it. This will be the top side of the platform. All inside corners of the frame and plywood are then sealed with a silicone rubber sealant.

Next, the locations of the air circulation holes that will be drilled in the plywood (see Plate 6) are laid out. These holes should be 3/8" in diameter. Now an air-inlet slot (of the same dimensions as the air outlet of the blower) is cut in one side of the platform frame. This slot is positioned so that it faces the door (in which the ventilation grill has been installed). Before the blower is attached, it is recommended that another piece of 1/2" plywood be nailed to the bottom of the frame. Then all outside corners of the frame and the plywood are sealed with silicone sealant. When the sealant has cured, the top and sides are painted with either a white latex semi-gloss or flat white paint. The brush should be kept fairly dry when painting, so that the air circulation holes do not become clogged.

Now it is time to attach the flange of the blower over the air-inlet slot on the frame. It is important to make sure that the platform is level. The platform must be positioned so that the blower is next to the ventilation grill on the door. This will allow the blower to draw a small volume of fresh air into the chamber. Since air is being pulled into the chamber, carbon dioxide will not be able to escape.

Because of the airtight condition of the chamber, excessive heat will build up and will have to be eliminated. If the air is continuously recirculated, the heat can be removed while maintaining the level of carbon dioxide in the chamber. A small 110-volt window-unit air conditioner is ideal for this application.

After installing the air conditioner in the window frame, it is necessary to seal around it tightly with a silicone sealant. The vent should be adjusted so that the chamber air will be recirculated. The thermostat is now turned to its lowest setting, the light switched on, and the room temperature allowed to stabilize. Then the thermostat is regulated until the desired temperature is reached. It should need to be adjusted only slightly, since the chamber temperature, on the average, will need to be reduced only 10 to 15 degrees. The air direction vents should be pointed away from the plants, so that the air delivered from the air circulation platform will not be interfered with.

Carbon Dioxide System

Presented here will be all the information necessary for supplying carbon dioxide to the growth chamber.

It is first necessary to calculate the volume of the growth chamber in liters. To do this, one must first find the number of cubic centimeters in the room. This can be done by one of two methods. The first is to measure the room with a meter stick. The second is to find the number of cubic feet and then convert to cubic centimeters. Since the most common measuring devices in the home are calibrated according to the English system, our example will calculate the volume in cubic feet, converting it into cubic centimeters and them into liters.

Assume the growth chamber is five feet in length, six feet in width, and seven feet in height. To calculate the number of cubic feet:

Length x Width x Height = Cubic Volume, or
5' x 6' x 7' = 210 cubic feet

Next, determine the number of cubic centimeters per cubic foot:

2.54 centimeters = 1 inch
16.39 cubic centimeters = 1 cubic inch
1,728 cubic inches = 1 cubic foot

$$1728 \frac{\text{cubic in.}}{\text{cubic ft}} \times 16.39 \frac{\text{cubic cm.}}{\text{cubic in.}} = 28,321 \frac{\text{cubic cm.}}{\text{cubic ft.}}$$

Calculate the total number of cubic centimeters:

$$28321 \frac{\text{cubic cm.}}{\text{cubic ft.}} \times 210 \text{ cubic ft.} = 5,947,620 \text{ cubic cm.}$$

Convert the total number of cubic centimeters to liters and obtain the final volume figure for the growth chamber:

1 cubic centimeter = 1 milliliter
1,000 milliliters = 1 liter
5,947,620 cubic cm. [div.sign] 1,000 milliliters = 5,948 liters

After the total volume in liters has been determined, the next step is to calculate the volume of CO_2 required.

As discussed above, the atmosphere contains approximately 300 parts per million of CO_2, and for our purposes, approximately 1,000 ppm above the atmospheric concentration is all we need for an optimalrate of photosynthesis. To calculate the proper amount of CO_2:

$$1 \text{ part per million} = \frac{10}{10^6} = 10^6$$

$$1{,}000 \text{ parts per million} = \frac{10^3}{10^6} = 10^{-3}$$

$$= .001$$

    $.001 \times 5{,}948$ liters (volume of the chamber) = 5.948 liters of CO_2, the amount required to produce 1,000 ppm per liter of CO_2 for the total volume of the chamber.

    Once the amount of CO_2 necessary for the total volume of the chamber has been determined, the delivery rate of the CO_2 regulator can be calculated. Many types of CO_2 regulators have adjustable, pre-calculated delivery rates; however, most of these are expensive, and they are not really necessary.

    For the accuracy that is required, a regulator used in beverage and beer-tap systems is more than adequate. The tank and regulator can be found at most bottled-gas dealers. If possible, the cheapest way is to rent both on a monthly basis. If this cannot be arranged, used tanks can be found at fire extinguisher companies; the price varies according to the size of the tank. Tank sizes range from a two-pound bottle to a sixty-five-pound one; the latter is the largest size one person can handle.

    When the tank and regulator have been acquired, make sure the tank is well-secured from falling before removing the safety cap, and attempting to attach the regulator. Care should be taken in connecting the regulator. The fittings must not be forced; this will cause the threads to be stripped. No lubricant may be applied; this will prevent a tight seal, and leakage will occur. The fittings should be tightened to hand tightness and the gas slowly turned on. Then the tightening is continued with a wrench until the leakage stops. Now a hose (of the type that will be described below for the water culture system) is attached, and the regulator is set at 15 pounds per square inch (psi).

    Next, a long cylindrical balloon must be blown up in order to calculate its volume. The volume (V) of a cylinder is $\pi r^2 h$, where π is equal to 3.14, r^2 is the radius (half the diameter) multiplied by itself, and h is the length of the cylinder. (These measurements should be made in centimeters.)

For example, suppose we have a balloon that measures 30 cm. in length when fully expanded. Its diameter is 10 cm., which makes the radius (half the diameter) 5 cm. Multiplying the radius by itself ($5 \times 5 = 25$) yields the value for r^2. The next step is to take these numbers and plug them into the equation $V = \pi r^2 h$:

$$V = 3.14 \times 25 \times 30 = 2{,}355 \text{ cubic centimeters.}$$

Remember that one cubic centimeter equals one milliliter, and that there are 1,000 milliliters in one liter. This means that by dividing 2,355 by 1,000, we find the volume of the balloon, which is 2.355 liters.

Now the balloon should be deflated and attached to the hose from the CO_2 regulator. The regulator must be set at 15 psi. The balloon is inflated again, and while filling it, a note is made of the time it takes to reach its original size. Let's suppose that the balloon takes 10 seconds to fill. We then know the delivery rate of the regulator to be 2.355 liters for every 10 seconds. Remember that the amount of CO_2 required to produce 1,000 ppm for the total volume of the room was 5.947 liters; this is approximately 2.5 times the volume of our balloon. Multiplying 10 seconds by 2.5, we find that it takes 25 seconds to deliver the amount of CO_2 that is necessary.

Continuous monitoring of CO_2 content would be ideal. However, gas analyzers and solenoid valves are necessary for continuous monitoring. Introducing CO_2 once every six hours during an 18-hour photoperiod would be adequate. In essence, any CO_2 that will raise the concentration above normal amounts will be beneficial.

Now the tank and regulator are placed outside of the growth chamber, as close to it as possible. The tank should not be placed in the room unless some kind of on/off valve device can be used from outside the chamber. If the chamber is opened while it is being filled with gas, the gas will simply dissipate into the surrounding atmosphere. Once the location is chosen, the tank is secured by any convenient means to ensure that it will not fall over. Next, a pathway into the chamber must be determined. The simplest method is to drill a hole the size of the hose and insert the hose into the room. Another hole should be drilled in the side of the air circulation platform, and the hose inserted through it. Both holes should then be sealed with a silicone sealant.

The CO_2 system is now complete. The timing sequence for entry of the carbon dioxide into the chamber will be given in the last section of this chapter.

Humidity Control Systems

The importance of relative humidity has already been discussed. The methods of controlling it will be presented in this section.

The most efficient way to control humidity is to use an automatic humidifier with a ten-gallon reservoir. This keeps the chamber at the desired relative humidity of 60 to 70 percent for several days at a time between refillings. Should a humidifier be too expensive, an alternative method is to use a pan of water. The pan must have a large surface area. It is placed in a corner with a small fan blowing over the surface toward the air circulation platform (never have any part of the body in the water when positioning the fan). This method is effective enough to produce a relative humidity of 30 to 40 percent. Yet another method is to spray the floor of the growth chamber with water (provided it is in a basement location). Although the humidity will not be even close to optimal, any increase in relative humidity over zero will be beneficial. If the latter method is used, be sure all electrical wiring is removed from the floor, and stay clear of any electrical connections while moving about the growth chamber to avoid potential electrical hazards.

With any of these methods, a hygrometer is necessary for checking the relative humidity in the chamber. It should be positioned on the wall of the chamber, in a place where it is readily visible and easily read.

Water Culture and Aeration System

Only one type of water pump should be used with the water culture system: the magnetic drive pump (see materials list). The inside diameters of the inlet and outlet of the pump should be 1", female-threaded. The pump must be air-cooled. (Any kind of submersible water pump is completely unsuitable. Submersible pumps raise the solution temperature high enough to literally cook the roots!) The flow rate of the pump for a four- to six-gallon growth tank system should not exceed 200 gallons per hour. If the flow rate is any higher there is a risk of overflowing the tanks.

As mentioned earlier in Chapter 2, there are three types of solution tanks: the growth tank, the constant-level tank, and the nutrient solution reservoir tank.

Growth tanks are ink buckets with lids, with a capacity of 1-1/2 and 2 gallons. Ideally, these buckets should be made of black polyethylene plastic. The carbon black pigment is chemically inert (will not react with and/or contaminate the nutrient solution). Moreover, black polyethylene is light-tight; remember that the entire system is made light-tight to prevent any algae or photosynthetic bacteria from contaminating the system. However, black is a good thermal conductor, which is undesirable, so the black plastic must be coated with a white glossy Epoxy paint. This will reflect the heat that would otherwise be absorbed by the black pigment, raising the solution temperature above acceptable levels. If black polyethylene buckets are unavailable, then white is the best substitute. White is less desirable because it must be made light-tight. (A method of doing this, along with the other procedures for the completion of the growth tanks, will be described in the section on construction.)

The constant-level tank is made from a four-gallon plastic dishpan (polyethylene if possible). If the dishpan is not light-tight, it must be made so. If System #2 is used (separating the nutrient solution reservoir tank and the constant level tank: see Chapter 2), a container larger than six gallons is suggested for growing no more than four plants. Ample reserves are then available during the photoperiod to prevent both water pump and plants from running dry. The tank is refilled before the beginning of the next photoperiod. With System #1, the float valve automatically refills the constant-level tank from the nutrient solution reservoir tank. With sufficient reserves in the solution reservoir tank, the system can run for short periods of time without being checked.

The constant-level tank must be covered. If it is not, the carbon dioxide supplied to the chamber will be dissolved in the solution, and will injure or kill the roots. Containers that cannot be obtained with lids must have lids constructed for them. (See the construction section for assembling both the constant-level tank and its lid.)

The nutrient solution reservoir tank should be a 5- to 10-gallon polyethylene barrel or jug. Black is preferable, but any color will do. If the tank is not light-tight, it should be made so. The coating of white Epoxy paint is not necessary for the nutrient solution reservoir tank. If the tank is positioned in a corner of the chamber, light intensities will not be high enough to affect the solution temperature. The tank must also be kept inside the growth chamber so that solution delivered to the constant-level tank will be at room temperature.

Three types of hoses are used in the water culture system: black neoprene rubber (for the solution feed hoses); green vinyl garden hosing (for the solution return and water pump hoses); and clear flexible vinyl (for the air inlet hose). The required length of each solution feed hose can be estimated by measuring from the growth tank location to the water pump. The water pump may be positioned in any convenient place, as long as it is outside the chamber. Another length of solution feed hose is needed to run from the nutrient solution reservoir tank to the float valve on the constant-level tank. Next, for the solution return hoses, it is necessary to measure from the location where the growth tanks will be located on the air circulation platform to the position of the constant-level tank (not more than two feet from the air circulation platform). The water pump inlet and outlet hoses are connected to the inside of the chamber through a hole near the bottom of the chamber wall. The length of the inlet hose is determined by measuring from the pump inlet orifice to the constant-level tank. For the outlet hose, measure from the pump outlet orifice to 12 inches inside the chamber wall. To estimate the length of air inlet hose required, measure from the location of the nutrient solution reservoir tank to the nearest point outside the chamber. The air inlet hose prevents a vacuum from occurring in the nutrient solution reservoir tank while solution is being delivered to the constant-level tank (necessary for both System #1 and System #2). It must be connected to the outside of the chamber to keep carbon dioxide from being drawn into the tank. When calculating the length of each hose, it is useful to add a couple of extra feet to work with.

Aeration System

The most important component of the aeration system is an aquarium air pump. There are many varieties; the one that is used should have enough air pressure to handle an under-gravel filter for an aquarium whose capacity is equal to that of the water culture system. Like the water pump, the air pump should be placed outside the chamber to prevent the carbon dioxide in the chamber from being pumped into the growth tanks.

A multiple air valve is necessary to regulate air pressure from the air pump to the growth tanks. The number of air valves required is equal to the number of growth tanks in the system. Air stones (the type used in aquariums) are also needed. The purpose of the air stones is to break up the air into small bubbles as it rises into the nutrient solution. The air is more readily dissolved in the water in this form; therefore, more oxygen will be present in the water for absorption by the roots. Air stones are rated coarse, medium, fine, and extra-fine. The fine or the extra-fine should be used if possible. A clear, flexible vinyl air hose is also necessary. This hose provides air from the air pump (outside the chamber) to the multiple air valve (inside the chamber, as close to the growth tanks as possible), and from the multiple air valve to each growth tank.

The necessary length of air hose can be calculated by measuring from the air pump position to the multiple air valve, and from the multiple air valve to the location of each growth tank. Again, it's useful to add a couple of extra feet to work with. (The construction section of this book may be consulted for details on the completion of the aeration system.)

Materials List for the Water Culture and Aeration Systems

Here is a comprehensive list of materials for construction of both the water culture system and the aeration system:

Tanks

Growth Tank Black or white polyethylene ink buckets with lids.

Constant-Level Tank Container made of polyethylene or equivalent, light-tight if possible, any color, with or without lid. For System #1, its capacity should be four gallons; for System #2, six to eight gallons.

Nutrient Solution Reservoir Tank Barrel or jug made of polyethylene or equivalent, light-tight if possible. Capacity should be between five and ten gallons.

Hoses, Tubing, and Couplings

Solution Feed Hoses 1/4" I.D. x 1/8" wall thickness, black neoprene rubber hose (predetermine necessary length).

Solution Return Hoses 3/4" I.D. x 1/8" wall thickness, green vinyl garden (predetermine necessary length).
Water Pump, Inlet & Outlet Hoses 3/4" I.D. x 1/8" wall thickness, green vinyl garden hose (predetermine necessary length).

Air Hose 3/16" I.D. x 1/8" wall thickness, clear flexible vinyl hose (predetermine necessary length).

Air Inlet Hose 1/4" I.D. x 1/8" wall thickness, clear flexible vinyl hose (predetermine necessary length).

Air Lines 1/8" I.D. x 12" length, clear rigid air tubing.

Hose Couplings Straight plastic hose couplings: 1/4" I.D. x 1-1/4" length (see below). One is necessary for each growth tank. One coupling is needed for the nutrient solution reservoir tank and one (1/2" I.D. x 1-1/4" length) is required for the constant-level tank.

"T" plastic hose couplings: 1/4" I.D. (see below). The number of "T" couplings necessary is determined by subtracting one from the total number of growth tanks.

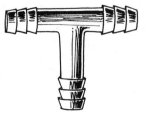

3/4" diameter male and female hose couplings: these are the type used for garden hoses (see below). Two male couplings are needed for each growth tank, four for the constant-level tank, three for the water pump inlet hose (this will have the foot valve connected to it and will be explained in the construction section), and one for the water pump outlet hose. For each solution return hose, two female couplings, one for each end (a total of 8 couplings), are required.

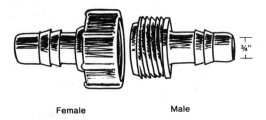

Female   Male

Hose reduction coupling: 2" in length, 3/4" I.D. at entry and 1/4" at exit; reduces the 3/4" I.D. of the water pump outlet hose to the 1/4" I.D. of the solution feed hoses (see diagram).

Rubber Stoppers

#00 with   One for each growth tank.
single hole

#4 with   One for each growth tank, two for the constant-
single   level tank, and one for the nutrient solution
hole   reservoir tank.

#10 solid   One for each growth tank.

Clamps

"C" Clamp   Three-inch throated. Necessary for keeping the lid held tightly onto the constant-level tank, even if the lid is made to snap onto the container. One for each corner and two for each side should be sufficient.

Screw Clamp   (See diagram.) Two that reduce to 1/4" are required, plus 14 that reduce to 5/8". Each will be discussed in the construction section.

Hose Clamp Clamps off the solution feed hose on the nutrient solution reservoir tank while hose is removed from the constant-level tank (see below).

Paint and Accessories

Flat Black Paint The type used should be Epoxy with a 30-second to 1-minute set time and a 10- to 15-minute drying time.

Glossy White Paint The type used should be Epoxy with the same set and paint drying times as the flat black paint.

Sandpaper Use 240-grade emery cloth for all painted surfaces.

Paint Thinner Any type.

Aeration Equipment

Air Pump Make sure that it has enough air pressure to handle an aquarium whose capacity is equivalent to that of the water culture system.

Multiple Air Valve Type used for aquariums. One is needed for each growth tank.

Air Stones Use fine or extra-fine grade.

Adhesives

Epoxy 5-minute: this type sets tack-free in five minutes and cures in 24 hours.

Patch   this type of epoxy has the texture of putty. It sets tack-free in 30 minutes and cures in 24 hours.

Silicone   Adhesive/Sealant: this type of silicone compound bonds better to plastic surfaces. Sets tack-free in 45 minutes and cures in 24 hours.

Water Purification Device

Polyester Fiber   Type used for aquarium filters.

Activated   Type used for aquarium filters.
Charcoal

PVC Tubing   4" I.D. x 4' in length.

Plexiglass/Lucite 5" x 5" square, 1/8" thick.

Funnel   Plastic, large enough to fit over the outside diameter of the PVC tube.

Water Pump

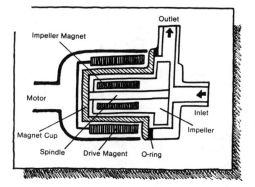

Magnetic Drive Pumps

Rather than shaft seals, which wear out and leak, magnetic drive pumps use magnetic fields to couple the motor to the pump impeller. Conventionally-coupled pumps have a shaft penetrating the pump head and seals to prevent leakage along the shaft. The shaft rotation will eventually wear out that seal, causing leakage.

Magnetically coupled pumps confine the liquid to a wholly enclosed chamber so no fluid can escape from the pump head. This eliminates dangerous spills of liquid and damage to motor components.

The illustration shows a typical magnetic drive pump with a centrifugal pump head. The motor is attached to a large cylindrical drive magnet. The magnet cup fits into the hollow of the drive magnet. The magnet cup forms the back portion of the pumping chamber. Inside the magnet cup is a smaller magnet riding on a spindle, attached to the impeller. As the large magnet rotates around the cup, the driven magnet/impeller assembly rotates within, turning at the speed of the motor. A static O-ring prevents leakage between the magnet cup and the front of the pump head.

No friction loss: there is no mechanical seal to cause friction and slow down rotation. All motor horsepower is transmitted to the impeller. This makes a magnetic drive pump more efficient than conventionally coupled pumps.

Miscellaneous Supplies

Drill Bits　　　3/8"; 1/2"; 5/8"; 1-1/4"

Float Valve Optional, depending on which system is used. Various types of float valves are available. For one type, see diagram below.

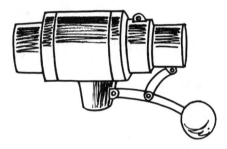

Foot Valve Type used should be PVC plastic with 1" female-threaded inlet and outlet holes (see diagram below). Prevents the backflow of solution from the growth tanks into (and ultimately overflowing) the constant-level tank, should the water pump stop working.

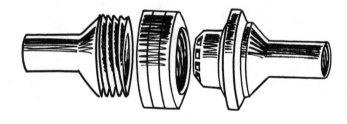

—— Water Flow Direction ⟶

Styrofoam Ball　　Used for the float on the float valve if one is not provided with the valve.

Male-threaded Variable Size Hose Adapter	Necessary for connecting the solution feed hose from the nutrient solution reservoir tank to the float valve. It also attaches the float valve to the constant-level tank. The male thread diameter is determined by the female thread diameter of the float valve (see diagram below).

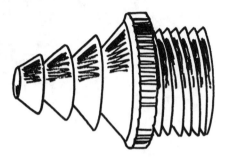

Plexiglass/ Lucite	Opaque white, 1/8" thick. Used for constructing the lid for the constant-level tank, if one is not available.
Weather Stripping	The same type used to seal the doors on the growth chamber.
Screen	Plastic with medium mesh. Used for making filters in the growth tanks and the constant-level tank.
Thermometer	Dial type, with 5-1/2" stem (see diagram below).

Funnel Plastic	Large enough to cover a 5/8" hole.
Teflon Tape	1/2" wide or narrower.

Exacto Knife   Surgically sharp blade.

Female-Threaded   These caps fit onto and seal off
Seal Caps   the 1" diameter threads on the   male-
    threaded hose couplings. One per growth
    tank.

24-Hour Appliance Three are required: one for the light,
Timer   one for the ventilation fan on the air
    circulation platform, and one for the air
    conditioner and humidifier.

All materials listed can be obtained at: hardware stores, plastic container companies, restaurant supply companies, adhesive companies, scientific and hobby supply stores, rubber companies, water pump dealers, and pet shops.

Construction of Water Culture and Aeration Systems

Growth Tanks

Step 1   The entire outer surfaces of the tanks and lids must be sanded with emery cloth. This will keep the paint from peeling off the surfaces.

Step 2   Wipe the surfaces with paint thinner and remove the excess with a clean cloth. Let the paint thinner dry for at least one hour. The surfaces are then ready to be painted.

Step 3   If the tanks are black polyethylene or light-tight plastic, go to Step 4. If not, apply several light coats of flat black paint to build up the necessary thickness and to prevent runs. The same applies to the lids. Allow the paint to dry for 24 hours.

Step 4   Paint the surfaces of the tanks and lids with white glossy Epoxy paint. Again, apply several light coats until the desired thickness is reached. Allow the paint to dry for 24 hours.

Step 5   Using the 5/8" drill bit, drill a hole in the center of each lid. Use the Exacto knife to enlarge the holes to a diameter of 1-7/8". Insert a #10 rubber stopper into each hole to ensure a tight fit.

Step 6   With the 5/8" drill bit, drill a hole about 1" from the edge of each lid. Place a #4 rubber stopper in each hole to ensure a tight fit.

Step 7   With the 3/8" drill bit, drill a hole in the side of each tank, as close to the bottom as possible (see Plate 9). Insert a #00 rubber stopper in each hole to ensure a tight fit.

Step 8   With the 5/8" drill bit, drill two holes in the side of each tank: one 6" from the bottom of each tank, and the other between 1" and 1-1/2" from the top (see diagram below).

Step 9   Roughen the inner and outer surfaces around the holes in the tanks with emery cloth (lightly on the outside).

Step 10   Wrap Teflon tape around the unthreaded ends of the two male-threaded hose couplings for each tank.

Step 11   Insert the male-threaded hose couplings in the 5/8" holes so that they catch between the barbs (see diagram below). It may take a great deal of force to get the barbs through the holes. If the holes must be enlarged, do so only slightly. The tighter the fit, the better the seal! Be careful not to force the hose coupling beyond the second set of barbs. If this happens, the coupling must be pulled out, and will usually crack the tank.

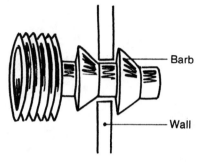

Step 12   When the couplings have been inserted, use a hair dryer to heat the inner surface of each tank around the couplings.

Step 13   Apply the Epoxy "patch" around the couplings and heat it with the hair dryer until it flows over the connected area (see diagram below).

Expoxy Patch

Step 14   Rest the tank with the couplings facing downward and allow it to cure for 24 hours (see diagram below).

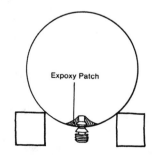

Expoxy Patch

Step 15   Repeat Steps 12 and 13 on the outer surfaces around the couplings. Rotate the tanks with the couplings facing up when curing the Epoxy (see diagram below).

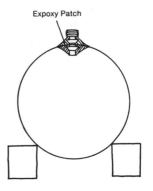

Expoxy Patch

Step 16   Apply the silicone adhesive/sealant over the Epoxy "patch" on both sides of the couplings. Extend it at least 2" beyond the termination point (see diagram below). Cure for 24 hours.

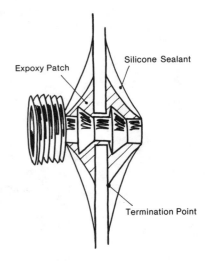

Expoxy Patch
Silicone Sealant
Termination Point

Step 17   To determine the length of screen necessary for the tank filter, measure from the top coupling to the bottom coupling and add 8". The width should be

6". Cut a two-inch square from each corner of the screen. Fold up the sides into a box. Wrap masking tape around the outside to hold it in shape. Using the 5-minute Epoxy, run a bead along each inside corner. Allow 15 minutes before removing the tape.

Step 18   Run a bead of silicone around the edge of the screen box and place it over the couplings on the inside of each tank (see Plate 10). Run another bead along the joint where the box and the tank meet. Make sure there are no gaps or spaces between the box and the tank.

Step 19   Wrap Teflon tape around the threads of both male-threaded hose couplings on the tanks.

Step 20   With a pair of pliers, hold the back sides of the couplings and screw the seal caps onto the male-threaded hose couplings that are 6" from the bottom of each tank (see Plate 11). Be sure to hold the couplings firmly with the pliers; if not, there is a likelihood of breaking the Epoxy-and-silicone seal.

A completed tank and lid should bear a rough resemblance to those shown in Plate 12.

Constant-Level Tank

Step 1   Same as Steps 1–4 for the construction of growth tanks.

Step 2   With the 5/8" drill bit, drill a number of holes across the length of one side of the tank, equal to the number of solution return hoses that will be used. These holes should be 3" apart and 2" from the top of the tank (see diagram below).

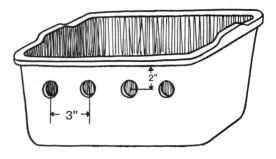

Step 3   Using the 5/8" drill bit, drill a hole in the side at one end as close to the bottom as possible (see diagram below).

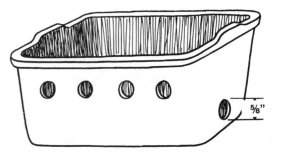

Step 4   Roughen the inner and outer surfaces around the holes with emery cloth (lightly on the outer surface).

Step 5   If the float valve is used, follow Steps 6–10; if not, go to Step 11.

Step 6   Drill the hole that will interface the variable-size hose adapter and the float valve to the tank, 2" to 2-1/2" from the top (opposite the end of the lower hole; see diagram below). The size of the hole is determined by the thread sizes of both the adapter and the valve.

Float Valve &
Hose Adaptor
Connection Hole

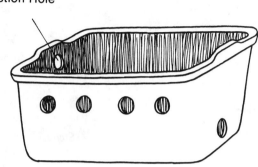

Step 7   Position a 2-1/2" I.D. washer between the float valve and the tank. Position another between the adapter and the tank (see diagram below). This gives support to the tank wall and prevents cracking.

Tank Wall

Washer

Washer

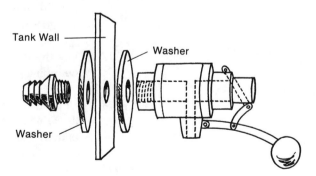

Step 8   Apply silicone around the hole between the two washers and the tank.

Step 9   Attach the adapter to the valve and tighten firmly.

Step 10   Allow the silicone to cure for 24 hours.

Step 11   Wrap Teflon tape around the unthreaded ends of the male-threaded hose couplings.

Step 12   Perform Steps 11-16 from the procedure outlined for the growth tanks.

Step 13   Cut a 4" square piece of screen and then cut one square inch from each corner. Fold into a box. Wrap masking tape around the outside. Apply 5-minute Epoxy along each inside corner. Allow the Epoxy to cure for 15 minutes before removing the tape.

Step 14   Run a bead of silicone around the edge of the screen box and place it over the 5/8" hole in the bottom of the tank. Run another bead along the joint where the box and the tank join. Make sure there are no gaps or holes between the box and the tank. Allow the silicone to cure for 24 hours.

Step 15   Wrap Teflon tape around the threads of the male-threaded hose couplings on the tank.

Step 16   If a lid must be constructed, follow Steps 17–21; if not, go to Step 22.

Step 17   Lay the top of the tank down on a piece of brown wrapping paper and trace around the outside edge.

Step 18   Cut out the pattern of the tank lid and tape it onto the white opaque Plexiglass. Now trace around the pattern with a grease pen.

Step 19   Remove the pattern and cut along the outside with a jigsaw.

Step 20   File the cut edges with a rasping file, then sand them with emery cloth.

Step 21   On one side, attach the weather stripping
along the entire edge of the lid (see Plate 13).
Use the Exacto knife for trimming.

Step 22   With the 5/8" drill bit, drill a hole in the
center and 4" from one end of the lid (see
diagram below; also, see Plate 13).

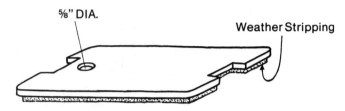

5⁄8" DIA.

Weather Stripping

Step 23   Insert the dial thermometer through a #4 single-
hole rubber stopper.

Step 24   Place rubber stopper with thermometer in the
5/8" hole to ensure a tight seal.

A complete constant-level tank should resemble Plates 14,
15, and 16.

Nutrient Solution Reservoir Tank

Step 1   If the barrel or jug is not light-tight, make it so,
using the procedure described in Steps 1–3 for
the growth tanks. If the tank is made of light-
tight plastic, it will not be necessary to paint it
with white glossy Epoxy paint. The tank will
be positioned in a corner of the room where
light intensity will not be a factor in raising
the temperature of the solution.

Step 2   In the center of the tank, drill a 5/8" hole (see diagram below).

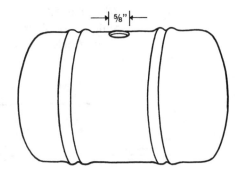

Step 3   Drill another 5/8" hole, exactly opposite the first hole (see diagram below).

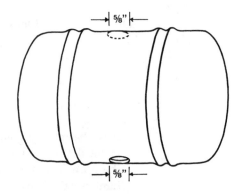

Step 4   Roughen the surface around only one of the holes with emery cloth.

Step 5   Lay the tank on its side with the roughened hole facing upward.

Step 6   Apply 5-minute Epoxy around the top of the funnel that will fit over the 5/8" hole.

Step 7   Place the funnel over the hole (see diagram below).

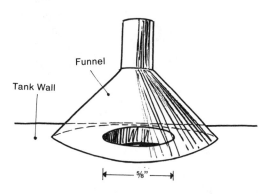

Step 8   When the Epoxy has set, heat the funnel with a hair dryer. Apply the Epoxy "patch" over the funnel up to the nozzle and down onto the tank 2" out from the edge of the funnel (see diagram below).

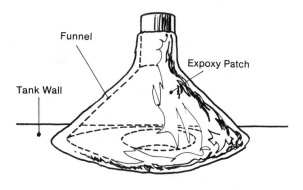

Step 9   Allow the Epoxy to cure for 24 hours.

Step 10   A support for the tank must be constructed to keep it elevated at least two feet above the constant-level tank. If the tank is round, a cradle similar to the one in Plates 17 and 18 may be used. However, any support will suffice as long as it allows the funnel to face downward and maintain the required distance from the constant-level tank.

Step 11 Place the nutrient solution reservoir tank on the cradle and insert the #4 rubber stopper with the straight plastic hose coupling into the 5/8" hole on top. Attach the air inlet hose to the couplings and run the hose to the predetermined location outside the growth chamber (see Plate 18).

Rubber Stoppers

Step 1 Place all four #10 stoppers, two of the #4 stoppers, and all four #00 stoppers in a freezer for 24 hours.

Step 2 Remove the #00 stoppers one at a time; use the 3/8" 3/8" drill bit to enlarge the single hole in each one.

Step 3 Insert the 1/4" I.D. x 1-1/4" long straight plastic hose coupling through the hole in the stopper, so that the end is flush with the surface of the stopper (see diagram below).

Step 4 Remove one #4 stopper from the freezer and with the 3/8" drill bit, enlarge the single hole.

Step 5 Repeat Step 3.

Step 6 Remove the second #4 rubber stopper and with the 5/8" drill bit, enlarge the single hole.

Step 7 Repeat Step 3, only insert the 1/2" I.D. x 1-1/4" long straight hose coupling instead.

Step 8 Repeat Step 2 with the four #10 stoppers, then place them in the freezer for another 24 hours. Repeat again, using the 5/8" and 1-1/4" drill bits.

Step 9   When the #10 stoppers have been drilled, cut one slit all the way through from the top to the bottom of each stopper (see diagram below). This will enable the stoppers to be removed from around the plants after they have been taken from the growth tanks.

Hoses

Solution Feed Hoses

Step 1   Repeat Steps 1, 2, and 4 from the procedure for growth tank construction.

Step 2   Attach the #00 rubber stoppers with the 1/4" I.D. x 1-1/4" long straight plastic hose couplings into one end of each hose.

Step 3   Cut the water pump inlet hose in two, six inches from the end of the hose. Take the 6" piece of hose and insert the #4 rubber stopper with 1/2" I.D. x 1-1/4" long plastic coupling into one end of the hose and secure with a screw clamp that reduces to 5/8". Into the other end, insert a male-threaded hose coupling and secure it with the same size hose clamp. Insert male-threaded hose couplings into each end of the other piece of hose, and secure with hose clamps that reduce to 5/8" (see diagram next page). Wrap all of the male-threaded hose couplings with Teflon tape.

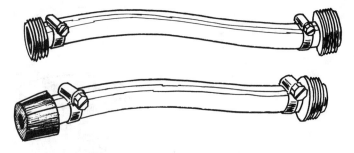

Solution Return Hoses

Step 1   Repeat steps 1 and 2 of the procedure for growth tank construction.

Step 2   Insert a female-threaded hose coupling into each end of the hoses and secure with a screw clamp that reduces to 5/8" (see diagram below).

Aeration System

Step 1   With the 5-minute Epoxy, bond an air stone in one air stone in one end of a 12" long rigid air tube.

Step 2   Allow the Epoxy to cure for 24 hours.

Step 3   Slide the other end of the rigid air tube through the hole in a #4 rubber stopper. Leave 2" above the top of the stopper (see Plate 19).

Water Purification Device

Step 1   Take the 5" x 5" square of plexiglass and place one end of the 4" diameter PVC tube on top of it (see diagram below).

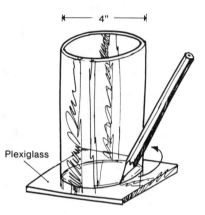

Plexiglass

Step 2   Trace around the outside circumference of the tube on the plexiglass with a grease pen.

Step 3   Cut out the circle with a jigsaw.

Step 4   With a 5/8" drill bit, drill a hole in the center of the Plexiglass plate.

Step 5   Using the 5-minute Epoxy, glue the plate to one end of the PVC tube. Allow 15 minutes to cure.

Step 6   Glue the funnel over the tube and Plexiglass plate with 5-minute Epoxy (see diagram below).

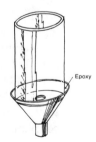

Epoxy

Step 7   Place a 2" thick layer of polyester fiber over the plate. Fill one-half of the tube with activated charcoal. Place another 2" of fiber over the top (see diagram below).

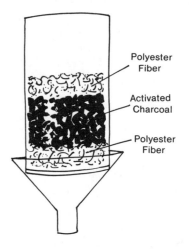

Polyester Fiber

Activated Charcoal

Polyester Fiber

Step 8   Place the water purification device in any suitable plastic container and fill with water. Keep filling the tube with water until the desired amount of water for storage is reached.

Assembly and Operation Procedures

Without its lid, place the constant-level tank with the male-threaded hose couplings facing, and not more than two feet away from, the air circulation platform. Then place the growth tanks (without lids) in their designated positions on the air circulation platform, with the male-threaded hose couplings on the growth tanks facing the constant-level tank (see Plate 20). Place the water pump in the position it occupied, outside of the growth chamber, when measurements for the inlet and outlet hose lengths were made. Attach both the water pump inlet and outlet hoses to the water pump. Run both hoses through the hole in the growth chamber wall to the inside of the room. Connect the longer section of water pump inlet hose to the foot valve. Attach the 6" piece of water pump inlet hose, with the straight plastic hose coupling and rubber stopper, to the foot valve, and then insert the rubber stopper into the 5/8" lower hole on the constant level tank (see Plate 21). Insert the 3/4" I.D. end of the 3/4" I.D. x 1/4" I.D. hose reduction coupling into the end of the water pump outlet hose and secure with a screw clamp that reduces to 5/8". For each "T" plastic hose coupling used in the system, minus one, cut a one-inch section from each solution feed hose. Connect the separate "T" plastic hose couplings together with the one-inch sections of solution feed hosing (see Figure 10). Connect all solution feed hoses to the "T" plastic hose couplings and insert the ends, with the straight plastic hose couplings and rubber stoppers, into the bottom of each growth tank. Connect the solution return hoses to the growth tanks and constant-level tank. Attach the solution feed hose that connects the nutrient solution reservoir tank to the float valve on the constant-level tank (if System #1 is used). Secure the end of the solution feed hose that is attached to the funnel on the nutrient solution reservoir tank with a screw clamp that reduces to 1/4". Place the aquarium air pump (outside of the chamber) and the multi-air valve (inside the chamber) in the locations they occupied when measurements were made for the length of the air hose that connects the air pump to the multi-air valve. Then use the air hose to connect the air pump with the multi-air valve. Attach the air hoses of predetermined length (which run from the multi-air valve to the growth tanks) to each valve on the multi-air valve. Connect the other end of each of the air hoses to the rigid air tubing (air line) with rubber stopper and air stone. The system has now been completely assembled and is ready for theoperation procedures.

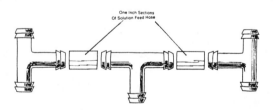

Figure 10. Remember, to calculate the number of "T" plastic hose couplings necessary, simply subtract 1 from the total number of growth tanks used in the system. For example, if four growth tanks were used, then three "T" plastic hose couplings would be needed. Then as mentioned, subtract 1 from the number of "T" couplings used in the system to obtain the number of 1" solution feed hose sections required. In this example, two 1" sections are necessary.

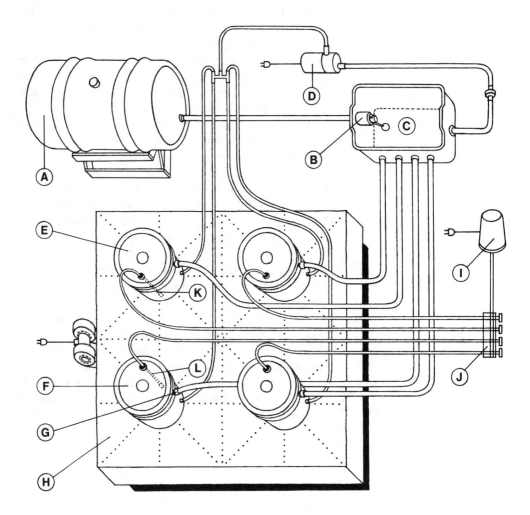

Prepare an amount of nutrient solution equal to the capacity of the system. (Use nothing larger than a three-gallon container when mixing the solution; a larger vessel would only increase the difficulty of handling the solution.) Disconnect the "T" plastic hose couplings from the 1/4" I.D. of the 3/4" I.D. x 1/4" I.D. hose reduction coupling. Fill the constant-level tank with nutrient solution to the bottom of the male-threaded hose couplings. Plug in the water pump (positioned outside of the growth chamber). Draw on the end of the water pump outlet hose with the mouth, very carefully so that water is not inhaled, this is to begin the siphoning action. Quickly reconnect the "T" plastic hose couplings to the hose reduction coupling and secure the screw clamp. This procedure is called "priming the pump"; it removes all trapped air from the pump head. This creates a vacuum, allowing the solution to be pumped. The function of the foot valve is this: if the water pump should stop running, or if the constant-level tank ran dry, a backflow of solution from the growth tanks to the constant-level tank would be prevented. Furthermore, it keeps air from re-entering the hoses and water pump head, eliminating the need to reprime the pump. As the solution level decreases in the constant-level tank, keep adding solution until it begins returning from the growth tanks, then add just enough solution to bring it up to the bottoms of the male-threaded hose couplings. The system should now be filled to capacity and recirculating. Plug in the aquarium pump; again be sure that no body contact is made with the water, and place the aeration tubes in their designated growth tank. (Do not insert the tubes into the growth tank lids at this point.) Adjust each valve on the multi-air valve so that the air flow is equal in all of the growth tanks. Now insert the aeration tubes into the growth tank lids. Place the lids over the growth tanks and constant-level tank, but do not attach them firmly yet. (See Plate 22.) Fill each #10 rubber stopper with a tight wad of polyester fiber, which will prevent the solution from evaporating into the atmosphere.

Take one 24-hour timer and set it for an eighteen-hour on/off photoperiod cycle. The cycle can be set for whatever schedule is convenient; however, remember that carbon dioxide must be injected into the growth chamber at the beginning of the photoperiod, and every six hours thereafter, if possible. Plug the timer into the electrical outlet with its separate circuit breaker (which should be on the outside of the growth chamber), and set the timer to the current time. Next, plug the light into the electrical outlet on the timer.

With the second timer, set the on/off cycle to match the photoperiod. Plug the timer into an electrical outlet in the growth chamber, being cautious of electrical hazards, and set the timer to the current time. Insert the two-way electrical adapter into the outlet on the timer. Plug the air conditioner and the ventilation blower into the adapter. Set the on/off cycle of the third timer to match the photoperiod. Carefully. Plug the timer into an electrical outlet in the growth chamber and set the timer to the current time. Plug the automatic humidifier into thetimer outlet. All individual systems are now functioning as a single environmental growth system, which should resemble Plates 23 and 24. The system should now be operated for one week. During this time, the solution and chamber temperatures should be monitored, as should the necessary adjustments to the air conditioner thermostat. Also check to make sure that the humidity is at the desired level. Check all connections throughout the system for leaks. Once the system has been checked for leaks and the desired temperatures and humidity levels have been reached, allow the system to stabilize until the end of the one-week test period. At this point, snap down the lids firmly on the growth tanks and clamp down the constant-level tank lid. The seedlings may now be placed in the growth tanks.

Remove the plants from their germinating media and rinse the roots off with water of the same temperature as the nutrient solution circulating in the system. Gently wrap polyester fiber around the stem just below the cotyledons. Be sure to wrap enough fiber around each plant to fill and seal the center hole in the #10 rubber stopper. Remove the polyester fiber previously placed in the #10 rubber stoppers and insert the plants in the growth tanks. The plants are now off and growing!

Note: If, after reviewing this chapter, readers decide not to go to the trouble of putting together their own water culture and aeration systems, a simpler route may be available. A prefabricated system would eliminate the purchase and assembly of materials. Those interested in obtaining additional information may write to the author in care of

H2O Plant Systems
P.O. Box 12732
North Kansas City, MO 64116

GLOSSARY

A

Algae: A group of primitive, chiefly aquatic, one-celled or multicellular plants that lack true stems, roots, and leaves. They usually contain chlorophyll, but may contain yellow, brown, red, purple, or blue-green pigments as well.

Alternation of Generations: A system in which the sexual and non-sexual phases of a plant's life cycle occur alternately. Found in certain algae, in a few fungi, and in all of the green land plants.

Anther: The top of the stamen, containing pollen at maturity.

Apical Meristem: The cells at the tip of a root or stem that are actively dividing.

Asexual: Reproduction by a single individual, not involving cellular or nuclear union with another.

Auxins: Plant hormones that are controlling factors in the upward growth of stems and the downward growth of roots.

Axil: The angle between the upper surface of the leafstalk (petiole) and the stem from which it arises.

Axillary Bud: A bud borne in the axil of the leaf.

B

Bacteria: Unicellular microorganisms, often forming sheetlike or filamentous colonies, existing either as free-living or parasitic organisms.

Bract: A modified or reduced leaf.

Bud: A minute stem, bearing the primordia of vegetative leaves.

C

Calyx: The collective term for the lowermost sterile appendages, usually green, on a floral receptacle (pistil).

Carbohydrates: Are divided into three basic food groups, each containing carbon, hydrogen, and oxygen only: (1)

sugars, which supply energy; (2) cellulose, which builds cell walls; and (3) starch, which provides food storage.

Carbon dioxide: A colorless, odorless, incombustible gas, which is heavier than air, formed during respiration, combustion, and organic decomposition. Necessary for carbohydrate production in plants.

Chlorophyll: Light-absorbing pigments necessary for photosynthesis.

Chloroplasts: Cellular structures that contain fats, proteins, and pigments (chlorophyll).

Chlorosis: Failure to produce normal amounts of chlorophyll.

Coenzyme: The optimum activity of many enzymes (though not all of them) depends on the cooperation of inorganic or organic non-protein substances called cofactors. The organic cofactors are usually called coenzymes. They are produced from vitamins, or in some cases are actually vitamins themselves.

Cotyledon: Primary embryonic leaf (monocotyledon), or leaves (dicotyledon).

Cytokinins: Plant hormones that stimulate cell division.

D

Desiccation: The process of becoming dry, dehydrated.

Differentiation: Initiating cells that develop into various tissue systems of the adult plant body.

Dioecious: If male and female flowers develop on separate plants of a given kind, that kind is said to be dioecious. See also Monoecious.

E

Egg: A large female gamete.

Embryo: An organism in the earliest stages of development.

Enzyme: A complex protein molecule, originating from living cells and capable of producing certain chemical changes in organic substances by catalytic action.

Epicotyl: The first bud and stem of a seedling sporophyte.

F

Fertilization: The union of egg and sperm in sexual reproduction.

Florigen: A plant hormone that stimulates flowering.

Flower: That part of a seed plant comprising the reproductive organs.

Fungi: A group of plants that have no chlorophyll. This group comprises the mushrooms, molds, mildews, etc.

G

Gamete: A sex cell that unites with another to form a zygote.

Germination: The growth and development of an embryo into a sporophytic plant.

Gibberillins: Plant hormones that are involved in both cell division and cell growth.

Glandular Trichomes: Unicellular or multicellular hairs. The head constitutes the gland, or secretory part, of the hair.

H

Hilum: A small pore at the end of the seed which is relatively permeable to water.

Hygrometer: A device for measuring relative humidity.

Hypocotyl: The first stem unit.

I

Inflorescence: An axis bearing flowers, or a flower cluster.

Internode: The region of the stem between two nodes.

M

Macronutrients: The essential elements that are present in the greatest quantities in plants. They are: nitrogen, phosphorus, potassium, calcium, sulfur, and magnesium. See Micronutrients.

Meiosis: A special type of nuclear division in which the diploid chromosome number (2n) is divided in half (haploid, 1n), and genetic segregation occurs. (Genetic segregation is the reshuffling of genetic material. When the chromosomes are split into two groups of 1n each, they are not exact copies of one another.)

Meristems: See Apical Meristem.

Micronutrients: Essential elements that are present in small quantities in plants. They are: iron, boron, manganese, copper, molybdenum, chlorine, zinc, and cobalt.

Mitosis: A kind of cell division in which the original number of chromosomes is preserved by replication, and segregation of the genes does not usually occur.

Monoecious: Where male and female flowers develop on the same plant, that kind of plant is said to be monoecious. See Dioecious.

N

Necrosis: Blackening and decay of tissues.

Node: The point of attachment of a leaf to a stem; also, the point of branch emergence.

Nucleic Acids: Ribonucleic acid (RNA) and deoxyribonucleic acid (DNA) are especially important, because they carry the information that determines what happens in a cell.

O

Ovary: In the pistil of a plant, the bottom portion which contains the ovules.

Ovule: The structure that contains the egg and eventually becomes the seed.

P

Petal: A colored, usually sterile appendage of a flower.

Petiole: The stalk that attaches the leaf blade of a plant to the stem.

pH: The concentration of hydrogen ions (H^+) in a solution is expressed as its pH.

Photoperiod: The relationship between the lengths of the day and night periods, which determines when flowering is initiated.

Photorespiration: Respiration that occurs in the presence of light.

Photosynthesis: The conversion of sunlight energy into food energy by green plants, i.e., those containing chlorophyll.

Phytohormones: Plant hormones; that is, auxins, gibberillins, and cytokinins.

Pigment: a coloring substance.

Pistil: The central seed-bearing organ of a flower.

Pollen Grain: A mature male gametophyte which contains the sperm.

Pollination: The transfer of pollen from the anther to the stigma.

Primordia: Tiny shoots in the earliest stage of development.

Proteins: Complex molecules built up by the union of many simpler molecules called amino acids. All living matter consists of proteins.

R

Radicle: The first root.

Reproductive Growth: In Cannabis, the point at which the onset of flowering signals the end of leaf production and the beginning of changes that culminate in seed production and in the death of the plant.

Respiration: In plants, a chemical reaction in which carbohydrates are broken down into carbon dioxide and water.

S

Sepal: The outermost leaves surrounding the flower; known collectively as the calyx. Sepals protect the inner parts of the flower in the bud.

Sexual: Reproduction involving nuclear union and meiosis.

Sperm: The mobile male gamete or male nucleus.

Spore: A reproductive cell which has the haploid chromosome number. Since it does not unite with others, it is not a sex cell.

Sporophyte: The spore-producing alternate of the alternating generations.

Stamen: Commonly thought of as being the male parts of the flower. They comprise a slender stalk, or "filament," and the anther.

Stigma: The pollen-receptive region of the pistil.

Stomate: A small pore in the epidermis of leaves, stems, fruits, and flowers, which allows for the exchange of gases between the plant and the air.

T

Transpiration: The loss of water from the plant in the form of water vapor through the stomates.

V

Vegetative Growth: The development of the sporophyte from seed germination to floral initiation.

Z

Zygote: A cell produced by the union of two gametes. This cell grows up to produce the sporophyte.

Rockwool Growing Medium
by George Cervantes

Rockwool is the neatest invention since the sun! It is an inert, sterile, porous, non-degradable growing medium that provides firm root support. Like all soilless mediums, rockwool acts as a temporary reservoir for nutrients. This affords the grower a tremendous amount of control over plant growth through nutrient uptake.

This revolutionary new growing medium consists of thin strand- like fibers made primarily from limestone, granite or almost any kind of rock. Rockwool has the appearance of lent collected by cloths dryer. It is unique and does not resemble any other growing media.

Rockwool has been used for many years as home and industrial insulation. In fact the walls in your home may surround you with this product. The rockwool used for insulation is very similar to the horticultural grade except for one thing; the industrial grade used for insulation is treated with a fire retarding substance that will kill plants.

Growers all over the world will be using rockwool as soon as they find out about it. Definite advantages are reaped when growing in this soilless substrate. It is economical, consistent and easy to control. Now the best part: rockwool is very fibrous in structure and will hold about 20 percent air even when it is completely saturated.

If this stuff is so good, why haven't I heard of it yet? Rockwool has recently been introduced into the U.S. in 1985. The word travels slowly and the American horticultural community has been slow to adapt. Most of them have not even heard of rockwool yet.

Rockwool has been used in European greenhouses for over 15 years. Rockwool was first discovered in Denmark in 1969. Growers began using rockwool as a way around the ban on soil-grown nursery stock imposed by some of the European community. Today, an estimated 50 percent of all western European greenhouse vegetables are grown exclusively in rockwool.

Other mediums like peat and soils are becoming more expensive to produce and can easily vary in quality.

This coupled with high cost of sterilization prompted European growers to explore new alternatives.

European growers switched to rockwool because it is inexpensive and easy to control but the important fact is that they not only changed, they continued to use it. More acreage is coming under production using rockwool daily. In fact growers at The Seed Bank in Holland swear by rockwool.

Rockwool is produced from rock alone or a combination of rock, limestone and coke. The rigid components are melted at temperatures exceeding 2,500 F. This molten solution is poured over a spinning cylinder, very similar to the way cotton candy is made with liquified sugar. As the molten solution flys off the cylinder, it elongates and cools to form fibers. These fibers could be likened to cotton candy fibers. The product of these fibers, rockwool, is then pressed into blocks, sheets, cubes or granulated. The blocks are rigid and easy to handle. They may be cut into just about any size desirable. Granulated rockwool is easily placed into growing containers or used like vermiculite or perlite as a soil amendment. The heat makes the rock wool sterile and I do not know of any bugs or microorganisms that are able to live at these temperatures.

Rockwool can be used in both recirculating and non-recirculation hydroponic systems. But the non-recirculating system is much easier to control. As explained earlier, the nutrient solution in a recirculating system is constantly changing. Salts soon build to toxic levels as plants use selected nutrients within the solution. The nutrient solution is constantly monitored and adjusted to provide the exact concentration of nutrients for optimum growth. However, with an open ended system, the excess nutrient solution drains off and is not recovered. The plants get all the nutrients they need and any nutrients that are not used will simply drain off. A fresh nutrient-rich solution is used for the next watering. Apply enough nutrient solution to get a 25 percent drain or leaching effect. This serves two purposes: 1) it flushes out excess salts from the medium and applies adequate nutrient solution to the medium.

When used with an open ended drip system, rockwool is easily irrigated with a nutrient solution controlled by a timer. The usual procedure in Europe is to apply a small amount of fertilizer to or three times a day. Enough excess solution is applied to obtain a 10–25 percent leeching effect every day.

Do not let all of this control fool you. Even though rockwool will hold 10–14 times as much water as soil, it does not provide the buffering action available in soil. The pH of rockwool is about 7.8. An acidic fertilizer solution (about 5.5 on the pH scale) is required to maintain the actual solution at a pH of about 6.5 or lower. Errors made in the nutrient solution mix or with pH level, will be magnified. Be careful to monitor both the pH and nutrient level with a scrutinous eye.

There are some tricks to handling rockwool. Dry rockwool can be abrasive and act as an irritant to the skin. When handling dry Rockwool, use gloves and goggles. Once the rockwool is thoroughly wet, it is easy and safe to work with; it creates no dust and is not irritation to the skin. Compaction is not a problem. Keep out of the reach of children and wash clothes thoroughly after prolonged use around rockwool as a safety precaution.

Rockwool stays so wet that algae grows on the surface. While this green slimy algae is unsightly, it does not compete with plants for nutrition, however harmless fungus gnats could take up residence. Abate this algae by covering the rockwool with plastic.

Horticultural rockwool is available from an ever increasing number of indoor garden stores. One of the main distributors is Wonderwool, 16521 Meridian Ave. N., Seattle, Washington 98133 Tel. (206) 542-4754. The owner, Greg McAllaster, is a fountain of knowledge and an expert on rockwool.

Computer Controlled Grow Rooms
by George Cervantes

Computer controlled grow rooms are rapidly becoming a reality. The technology is inexpensive and available. Following the leading edge of technology is the "trailing edge" of technology. This "trailing edge" is manifested in such affordable inventions as the personal computer, and sophisticated measuring and translating devices.

We are approaching a new era of affordable switches that take care of interfacing home computers to sensors of all kinds. These switches allow operation of remote devices under the control of a simple computer program. About the size of a modem or telephone these switches provide a means for the computer to communicate with the sensors it needs to read and the devices it will control.

Any computer with a standard RS-232 (serial) communications port and can control programs written in any language that can access a serial port will run the switch.

A computer has three main functions: input, processing and output. Input is acquiring the data, the information, temperature readings, measurements of CO_2, oxygen and moisture etc. The input can be "input" via a typewriter keyboard or console. This input is then "processed" by the computer. The processing generates "output": reports, graphs and charts.

In order for the computer to be able to receive input, it must be in a form that the computer can understand. With access to the data that is not normally read by computers, the processing is phenomenal. The computers must be able to read raw data directly form the input sources like thermometers, hygrometers, moisture meters, photoelectric cells, motion detectors etc.

Once the computer receives this data and is able to process the information, it should be able to generate some kind of "output" based on the information it received. The computer receives input, processes (makes a decision based based on the input) then generates a reaction or "output" to the solution. If it is too cold in the grow room, the heat will be turned on. If the soil is too dry, the water will be turned on.

The "output" function controls the grow room. A simple BASIC program to control temperature and moisture would be:

READ temperature READ moisture IF temperature is less than 70 THEN turn off heat IF temperature is greater than 80 THEN turn off heat IF moisture is less than 200 THEN turn on sprinklers IF moisture is greater than 300 THEN turn off sprinklers

The RS-232 communications port is one standard feature nearly all home computers have. With this standard feature in mind, technitions were able to design and market data acquisition devices for personal computers where there is a large potential market.

The two main types of data available from the measuring devices are digital and analog. Digital is the only one the computer can understand, but most of the raw data input comes in the analog form.

Digital outputs come two ways: ON or OFF. This is fine for many applications that can be answered YES or NO. For example in a security system, only needs to know if an area has been violated or not. If it is open, an area has ben violated. If not, all is secure. Whenever the question involves whether something is "on" or "off," it can be represented by digital data.

Measurements such as temperature, pressure, speed, humidity, acidity, distance, and many others may depend on the interpretation of analog data. Analog measurements can answer not only the question of "Yes or no?" but also the question "How much?" They do this by analogy, thus the similarity in terms. When we say something is three inches long, what we're really saying is that the object is "like three times the width of the king's thumb." If we refer to a temperature in degrees Celsius, we're saying that it is some fraction of the way between the temperature at which water freezes and the temperature at which it becomes steam. Thus we use the analogy of water freezing to determine the zero index for this analog temperature scale.

Many many very important measurements can only be made with analog data. But home computers only understand digital input and are able to output information digitally. The analog information must be broken down into a digital code bits and bytes that a computer can understand. When this analog data is translated into digital code, we call it digitizing.

The analog/digital conversion provides input to the computer program and the control function allows the computer to "do something" with the results of its processing.

Usually the control function serves to turn another device on or off as in the case of the temperature being too cold, the heat is turned on. More complex functions include digital outputs into various levels of response. Opening a vent to provide the right air circulation. Most often, output from the computer is used to turn current to digital outputs (to which electronic or mechanical relays can be connected) on or off. The relatively small currents processed by the ADC can control even large industrial motors or generators.

Need to know more about being able to make many devices available to the ADC.

Above and beyond looking after the grow room, the computer can easily monitor several areas of the house for security, check for signals from a fire or smoke detector, dial a close friend or dial you on your remote beeper. You could return the call to the computer, and listen to a pre recorded message or have a code number that the beeper dialed you to let you know the scope the disaster. The codes could range to anything from a lack of fertilizer in the nutrient solution to a burglar breaking into your home.

The concept of a "smart" thermostat, humidistat or photo electric cell is commonplace. With simple programming, the computer can measure the temperature in all areas of the grow room, determine how to bring the entire grow room to the predescribed temperature and control all kinds of heating cooling devices accordingly.

For security, a program can be written to simulate someone being at home during vacations. Turning lights, radios and appliances on and off.

A fire at your home could be as disastrous, unless the home is burned to the ground and the garden goes up in smoke as well. If the fire department shows up early enough to save the house, then they will undoubtedly find the indoor garden. One fireman from the Willamette Valley was fighting a fire when his own home caught on fire due to a faulty circuit in his halide. He had to leave the department and move to another town.

In a greenhouse equipped with an analog to digital converter (ADC), moisture, humidity, temperature, CO_2, whatever, can easily be controlled from a remote location. While you are gone, the computer will always do the same job every time. It will not daydream or get too loaded and fall asleep in the warm grow room. The computer does not make mistakes like a human operator does.

Remote Measurement Systems is one of the pioneers in developing an affordable analog/digital acquisition and control (ADC) systems. For a more complete, in depth information about the ADC switches, contact Remote Measurement Systems, Inc., 2633 Eastlake Ave. E. Suite 206, Seattle Washington, 98102, (206) 328-2255.